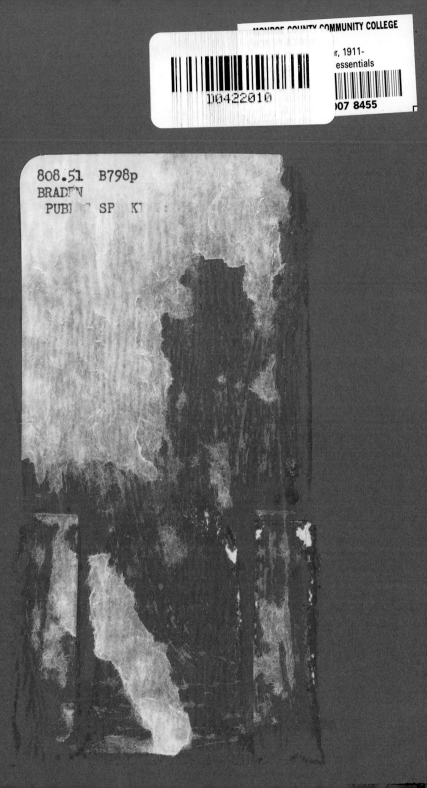

PUBLIC SPEAKING

Louisiana State University

PUBLIC SPEAKING
The Essentials

✺✺✺✺✺✺✺✺✺✺✺✺✺✺✺✺✺✺✺✺✺✺✺✺

WALDO W. BRADEN
Louisiana State University

✺✺✺✺✺✺✺✺✺✺✺✺✺✺✺✺✺✺✺✺✺✺✺✺

HARPER & ROW, PUBLISHERS, NEW YORK

Cover Photo George Zimbel from Monkmeyer

Library of Congress Catalog Card Number: 66-10318

CONTENTS

PREFACE

This book attempts briefly, pointedly, and simply to present the basic principles of speechmaking from the selection of a subject through the delivery of a completed speech. And that is all. It makes no pretense of offering an exhaustive treatment of rhetorical principles and practice. The book concentrates on the practical instead of the theoretical, and on the specific instead of the general. In many instances it offers no more than an introduction and an expanded outline, but it is intended to set the guidelines to rhetorical effectiveness.

Any well-conceived textbook should serve as a springboard to further inquiry and analyses, and as motivation for continued development. Stemming from a philosophy similar to that expressed in *Speech Practices* (Harper & Row, 1958), this book encourages the student to go beyond its pages to study speechmaking inductively, observing how others meet the problems of oral communication. The questions for investigation, the assignments, and the resource readings are designed to achieve these purposes.

The book may be used in three ways:

First, it may serve as the textbook in a brief, beginning-terminal, public-speaking course which places major emphasis on performance and constructive criticism.

Second, it may be used for longer courses with a supplementary textbook such as *Speech Practices, A Resource Book for the Student of Public Speaking*, an anthology of speeches, or a collection of "common materials."

Third, it may serve for a short adult course, refresher instruction, and industrial-communications training.

In assembling materials and ideas for this book, the author owes much to those with whom he has collaborated in the past, particularly Giles W. Gray, Earnest Brandenburg, and Mary Louise Gehring. These joint associations have contributed richly and materially to the author, and therefore to the present work. *Public Speaking: The Essentials* represents a fresh analysis, but it is necessarily related to, and in some instances draws heavily from, other books on which the author has worked.

The author wishes to thank Lorraine Allen for the illustrations and Beverly Van Sandt for assisting with the typing.

W. W. B.

October, 1965

PUBLIC SPEAKING

I

YOUR APPROACH
TO SPEECHMAKING

Many students of public speaking are surprised to learn that, as early as 467 B.C., an old Greek by the name of Corax established himself as a teacher of public speaking (or *rhetoric,* as it was referred to at that time) in the Greek city-state of Syracuse on the island of Sicily. Little information remains about this early teacher except that he wrote what was probably the first public-speaking text book—now lost—and that he had a famous pupil, Tisias. It is known, however, that about 20 years earlier, tyrants from a neighboring city-state, Gila, had overrun the citizens of Syracuse, seizing their lands and thus confusing the records of original ownership. When democracy was established about 465, the citizens had to go to court to untangle the ensuing disputes. Since there were no lawyers, the citizens were forced to plead their own cases. They learned—the hard way—that the fluent man was better able to win his way and to establish his claims than was the inarticulate and tongue-tied citizen. That discovery brought Corax many eager pupils, and systematic training in the art of communication has continued to be in demand ever since.

Today, many seek help in developing their oral abilities. Within a single year, the department of speech of one large university receives calls to give special training in speechmaking to such diverse outside groups as foremen of a large public utility, petroleum engineers, police officers, nurses, and cosmetologists. In order to meet this large demand, this speech department provides special student classes in addition to those regularly scheduled as a part of the curriculum. The same is true of many departments of speech through the country. Further, a large pharmaceutical firm has established its own speakers' bureau just to spread its public-relations' message abroad. This bureau is currently averaging 200 talks a month; its 500 trained speakers have already told their story more than 8,000 times to more than 340,000 persons. This instance is only one of many such programs carried on by business and industry.

In other words, more and more people, in a wide variety of jobs, are finding a knowledge of public speaking to be indispensable. As Clarence B. Randall—former President of Inland Steel, and Special Assistant to President Eisenhower on Matters of Foreign Economics —expressed it:

I claim that the educated man today must have a capacity for the communication of ideas. It is not good to be wise and learned if a man cannot do anything with what he knows and what he thinks. The educated man must be able to write and speak the English language convincingly, in order that his ideas may be communicated to others. Only then may he pull his weight in the community in which he lives.[1]

[1] Clarence B. Randall, "Liberal Education and the Challenge of the '60's," Address delivered at The Carleton College Dinner, Chicago, Ill., April 27, 1960. Published by Carleton College, Northfield, Minn.

Fig. 1.1. Many industrial corporations have established their own speakers' bureau to spread their public-relations messages.

Thus, when you decide to study public speaking, you are engaging in an important activity which can mean much to you in the future.

HOW TO STUDY PUBLIC SPEAKING

Departments of speech sometimes receive requests for correspondence courses in public speaking. Those who send such inquiries have a misconception about learning this subject. During the past 2000 years, the formal instructor of public speaking has usually incorporated the following elements:

1. Principles
2. Speaking Exercises

3. Listening Experience
4. Criticism

Omit any one of the four, and instruction becomes sterile, the student one-sided. Here, at the beginning of your study, you need an overview of how to study this subject.

Principles

James McBurney, Dean of the School of Speech, Northwestern University, observes that "an understanding of basic principles enables the speaker to profit by the best experience of others. . . ."[2] You will learn the principles in this course through the study of the textbook and the outside readings, from the lectures (probably fewer in number), and the comments of your instructor. In addition, you will want to seek answers to why certain practices work and under what conditions you should adopt them.

You should study your textbook the same way you approach any other subject. Because much of the class time will be filled with speaking exercises, you probably will be responsible for mastering the textbook on your own; very likely your instructor will not take class time for lengthy discussions of what you read because he will want to spend his time giving meaningful criticism of speaking performances. He will attempt to design exercises which will require you to *apply* the principles presented in the assigned reading material. Before preparing a speech, carefully consider what new principles have been presented in the recent assigned reading for application. You will probably be tested on the principles. Understanding the textbook is likely to weigh heavily in determining your final grade.

At the close of each chapter in the present text are included several questions for thought and discussion. Your teacher may ask you to investigate a given question and to report your conclusions to the class. Each question grows out of the material found in the chapter, but generally the complete answer is not found in a given

[2] James McBurney, "Fact and Fancy . . . ," *A Report of the Conferences on the Improvement of Writing and Speaking, The University of Missouri Bulletin,* **56** (November 15, 1955), pp. 23–30.

Fig. 1.2. Mastery of principles of public speaking requires thorough study of the textbook and further reading as well.

paragraph or even within the chapter as a whole. Thus, in many cases, you will need to do further reading beyond the present textbook to answer a question fully and intelligently. In other words, the questions should be regarded as springboards to further exploration of speech principles. You should think of yourself as a *searcher*, not just an *absorber*, if you are properly to grasp the principles of public speaking.

Speaking Exercises

The person who seeks a correspondence course in public speaking is probably under the erroneous impression that study of principles is sufficient to develop oral effectiveness. To the contrary, as much as 75 percent of class time may be devoted to student *performance*. It is as much through practice of oral delivery that effective speaking is mastered, as through study of theoretical principles. By practice we refer not only to performance itself, but also to the various preparation stages that lead up to the presentation.

Before speaking to your classmates you must plan carefully what you intend to say. Waiting until the last minute to prepare will not give you sufficient time to develop your remarks, to rehearse them, to maturate all the elements of the speech, or to give yourself an opportunity to develop confidence in what you want to say.

Let us enumerate seven important steps in speech preparation:

1. Analyzing the listeners
2. Selecting and limiting a subject
3. Preparing a plan or outline
4. Gathering supporting materials
5. Polishing your language
6. Mastering your speech for presentation
7. Oral rehearsal

Listening Experience

In participating in a public-speaking class, you will be a listener and observer more than you are a speaker; the same is certainly true in everyday living. Does this fact mean that the period between your speeches is wasted? Not at all! You can gain much from studying how your colleagues meet the assignments and cope with challenges of the class, and from what your instructor says about each presentation. In fact, each speech provides you with the opportunity to gain information and, at the same time, to continue to analyze your classmate and his experiences.

Therefore, your faithful class attendance is *necessary* and *important*. Although you may find real enjoyment in each assignment, you can also help your classmates to improve; by your overt attitudes

Fig. 1.3. Much of the class time will be devoted to practice through student performance. Even when you are not the speaker, you can gain valuable information through observation of your classmates' performances.

and facial reactions you can encourage each student when he speaks. Give to each speaker the same kind of attention that you crave when you are before the class. For example, if someone seems nervous or ill at ease, take care before you show disgust or laugh at a mistake. Remember, soon he will be *your* listener. As you hear him present his thought, ask yourself, "What must *I* do to hold *his* attention and interest?" Further, because you have a student's point of view, you can contribute to the class helpful suggestions concerning the elimination of faults and the mastery of principles. After class, give a fellow student a deserved compliment and let him know that you profited from or enjoyed his talk.

In this way, many classes develop great *rapport* among their members. Before the close of the term you will know personally each classmate, a unique experience in many college and university classes. You will come to appreciate one another's problems as well as aspirations. Members enjoy communicating with each other about mutual problems, and they take pride in each other's progress. When it is all over, you will have a circle of new friends, and you will remember each other for a long time. When this type of group dynamics occurs, progress for all concerned is rewarding and satisfying.

Criticism

Seeing yourself as others see you is also very important in your development as a speaker. When you take a public-speaking course or attempt to improve through study and practice, you are making a study of *yourself*, as well as of your speaking and of how listeners react to you. To practice the necessary objectivity required to see themselves is difficult for most persons because they are eager to see themselves as they would *like to be* instead of how they *really are*. You need a critic, a person of good will who is willing to observe and to discuss with you honestly what he sees and hears. But will you let a critic—a real critic—help you? "Ay, there's the rub."

At the mere thought of having a speech "criticized," some novices shrink with apprehension. Their self-conscious attitudes make the teacher's critical role indeed frustrating during the first days of a speech class. Bear in mind that the teacher wishes to help you, but, at the same time, he must protect you from yourself; he realizes that to tell you what you ought to hear may increase your speech fright, but to postpone revealing your weaknesses will only delay your march toward effectiveness.

In order to help you think more objectively about criticism, please consider carefully the following four suggestions:

1. *You need to develop, if you do not already have it, a wholesome attitude toward criticism.* Instead of fearing or dreading—or even resenting—what your teacher may say about your delivery, you should eagerly seek his suggestions. In fact, you should *insist that he tell you how to improve.*

2. *It is important that you understand the criticism itself.* Your instructor has the responsibility of making his feelings about your

speeches clear, and if he does not, that is his fault. But you, too, have a duty. If you do not understand his suggestions, seek additional information; for if you do not ask or listen, that is *your* fault. If you feel embarrassed about asking questions in class, make an appointment for a personal conference.

3. *Avoid emotionalized self-defense and rationalization when a fault is pointed out.* Some students fail to improve because they are continually trying to explain or to dismiss their failures. They rationalize with such excuses as:

"I didn't have time to prepare."
"The teacher picks on me."
"The teacher (or the class) dislikes me."
"I can't be expected to do as well as the others in the class."
"If I really wanted to, I could improve."
"I am much better than some of those the teacher compliments."
"The teacher does not know a good speech when he hears one."
"It isn't worth the effort anyway."

The student who fails to see through his own rationalization and to transcend his emotional defenses against honest criticism is unlikely to become a convincing speaker.

4. *Avoid developing a feeling of hopelessness or futility.* Some students apparently believe that they will have learned all there is to know about speaking in two or three weeks; when they fall short of this goal, they want to give it up as hopeless. Preparing, practicing, and presenting a speech is not something you can master in ten easy lessons; it requires time and effort. You will find that gaining proficiency in oral communication is sometimes slow, and that years of study go into the making of a truly great speaker. How much and how fast you develop will depend upon your native ability, your eagerness to improve, your willingness to work, and your receptivity to criticism.

The wise critic has an important function in your growth. In planning the course, your teacher has included exercises that will encourage you to develop sound practices. When he hears you speak, he will attempt to ascertain how well you are applying the principles and in what ways you need direction and encouragement.

He will attempt to lead you to substitute good habits for bad ones. Although the amount of time that he can devote to each speech will depend on the size of your group, you should look forward to his criticism.

Remember that your instructor is really interested in your improvement, and that it is a privilege to have your speech evaluated by him. His suggestions are designed to help you become an effective speaker.

CONQUERING YOUR FEARS

You may be willing enough to face up to and to accept criticism, but still have serious reservations about ever being able to face a large group of listeners. Your fear of speaking before an audience is anything but a private affliction of your own. It is experienced by professional as well as novice speakers.

An anxious mother sought advice from a columnist who promised to answer "questions on personal problems":

Perhaps you may be able to help me. I am an officer in our P.T.A. Days before the meeting I get so upset. The thought of getting up before all of the other mothers and reading the minutes makes me so nervous, I shake all over. Days before the meeting I can't sleep. If I resign my little girl will want to know why. How can I overcome my fears?

A Reader in Need [3]

When faced with the prospect of reading the Bible to 48 ministers, Charles Laughton, a famous actor and motion-picture star, reported "a painful case of stage fright." In spite of the fact that he had spent hundreds of hours on the stage and before the camera and in fact he had interpreted the great classics for thousands, he quaked at the thought of reading to a room full of preachers; he became more apprehensive as he speculated about his probable reception.[4]

[3] *St. Louis Post Dispatch*, April 15, 1952.
[4] Florabel Muir, "An Actor Discovers the Bible," *Saturday Evening Post*, **218** (November 24, 1945), p. 11.

The fact that stage fright took its toll of the little girl's mother and of the great actor offers proof that fear is no respecter of position or even of experience. There is hardly a speaker of prominence alive who has not experienced self-consciousness, who is not well aware of the symptoms: dryness of mouth, shaking knees, sweaty hands, shortness of breath, pounding heart, and even a queasy stomach. Sometimes three-fourths or more of the beginners in a public-speaking class report that what they want most from the class is to conquer their speech fears. In a study of 789 students at the State University of Iowa, Greenleaf found that 89 percent experienced some degree of stage fright, 32 percent thought their attacks were "mild," 47 said they were "moderate," and 10 percent mentioned "severe." Only 11 percent reported no fears.[5]

"Stage fright" is probably not a good name for this phenomenon because the victim does not have to be on a stage. It can happen almost any place. It resembles the sensation that one may have on a football field just before the opening whistle, on a deer stand as you wait for a great buck to gallop by, in a class when you merely ask a question, or when you recite a Bible verse at Sunday school. Fear—any kind of fear—results from what is unfamiliar, and what is not understood. In this course, you will have an opportunity to analyze this unpleasant experience and to see how it affects you. As you study your reactions, you will discover that many of your fears will disappear. Let us review several observations about fear on which many authorities seem to agree.

First, stage fright is a *normal* reaction; persons who have it are not abnormal or in any way handicapped. As the examples cited indicate, you are not alone if your voice shakes or your memory fails you as you stand before an audience.

Second, "stage fright" seems to have many origins, and no two persons are alike on what is likely to cause their fear of an audience. Here are some reported causes:

1. Inexperience in facing listeners
2. Belief that a beginner should be afraid
3. Habit resulting from conditioning yourself to experience fear

[5] Floyd I. Greenleaf, "An Exploratory Study of Speech Fright," *Quarterly Journal of Speech*, **XXXVIII** (October, 1952), 326–330.

4. An unpleasant past experience—e.g., having once forgotten a poem during Friday afternoon recitation
5. Fear of ridicule or censure
6. Over-eagerness to succeed
7. Failure to attain unrealistic goals
8. Lack of preparation
9. Desire to escape from the occasion

Third, listeners seldom judge the degree of fear to be as severe as the victim does. The harried speaker frets unnecessarily about how his listeners will react to him. When rating the severity of stage fright on a scale of 1 to 10 (10 representing the greatest intensity), the listeners are likely to give scores of only 3 or 4 to a speaker who assigns himself ratings of 7 to 9. A little objective observation of your classmates' responses to your performances will demonstrate that the overt manifestations are generally less obvious than you think. The self-conscious person is likely to focus on himself at moments when he should be concentrating upon his subject and how to make it clear.

Fourth, the beginner suffering from stage fright does give his listeners cues which distract somewhat from what he says. For example, he may develop a nervous laugh or some other annoying mannerism—like pulling an ear lobe—or an unpleasant voice pattern. When he avoids such signals, he becomes more communicative.

Fifth, systematic analysis of the nature and causes of stage fright seems to lessen its occurrence and severity. Almost any fear begins to disappear as you begin to understand it. Probably you should not strive for a complete *cure*, but you should concentrate on developing a positive outlook. You have stage fright because you have two wonderful abilities: the power to *remember* and the power to *anticipate*. You would not consider parting with these two attributes; a better solution is to learn how to turn them toward creativeness.

Sixth, stage fright lessens with experience before listeners and with familiarity with speaking situations. Frequent successful appearances build confidence, and confidence begets confidence. Novices who work faithfully in a speech class soon ignore or forget their fears; consequently, they encounter fewer symptoms as they continue to participate in class activities.

Some Suggestions for Controlling Your Fears

Concentrate on your subject—not yourself. Josephine Berosini, high wire artist of Ringling Brothers, Barnum and Bailey Circus, says that she never allows herself to be afraid when she walks the tight wire fifty feet about the ground. "If I allowed myself to be afraid I could never go up," she explains.[6] Good advice for a speaker! Do not *allow* yourself to be afraid. Stop thinking about yourself; put all your time on developing an eagerness to speak on your subject.

Careful preparation will save you embarrassment. When you know all about your subject, and when you have rehearsed it several times orally, you are better able to face your listeners. A later chapter treats speech preparation but, for the present, remember that knowing your material is a first step toward building your confidence. Do not memorize your speech; instead, practice it orally several times. Plan carefully the opening sentences which initial stage fright may make difficult. Include in your strategy the use of charts, models, and demonstrations in order to give you things to manipulate and thereby to release tension.

However, practice does not necessarily make perfect; it only makes permanent. Do not labor under the misconception that all you need to do to develop proficiency in speechmaking is to put in a certain number of appearances before listeners. To repeat a bad habit reinforces it and makes it more difficult to eliminate; and since bad habits will only lessen your effectiveness as a speaker, you cannot hope to gain confidence unless you keep an open mind to your own faults, and to criticism of them.

THE ELEMENTS OF THE SPEAKING SITUATION

With a basic, solid attitude toward the study of speech-making, you are now ready to begin building an understanding of the principles of public speaking. Speaking in public involves the interaction of four important elements:

[6] *Christian Science Monitor*, May 17, 1955.

1. The speaker
2. The speaking environment
3. The listeners
4. The speech

The speaker must adapt his message to his listeners as he and they interact within the speaking environment. *Interaction* is the important word. In other words, you must be aware of what is happening around you in order to gain a sympathetic reception for your remarks.

INTERACTION

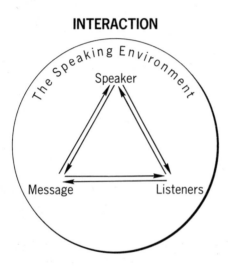

Fig. 1.4   *Interaction* is the important word.

Remember, that effective speaking results from thoughtful analysis, a sensitivity to listener attitudes, and the ability to adapt to whatever circumstances arise.

You As Speaker

What do the listeners have a right to expect of you as speaker? To put this question another way, how should you regard yourself when you ask people to listen to what you have to say? In commenting on the speaking of Lord Chatham, Lord Rosebery concluded, "It is not merely the thing that is said, but the man who says it that counts, the character which breathes through the sentences."[7] What kind of character "breathes" through your remarks?

Tennyson has Ulysses say, "I am a part of all that I have met."[8] So it is with the speaker. When you speak you reveal yourself. What you say reflects on where you have been, what you are, and what you want. The egocentric performer is generally a show-off who exploits speech-making to attract attention and to win admirers. Such a person has little to communicate—except himself. It is usually the case that this type has no right to ask for respect from his listeners.

As a speaker, you will do well to think of your listeners. In spite of the advice given by some popular manuals, you will find it best to be honest with your listeners about yourself and about your knowledge of your subject. As Albert J. Beveridge, political leader and an eloquent speaker, advised "Speak only when you have something to say. . . . Have ever in mind Carlyle's dictum that nobody has a right to speak in public unless he is so charged with the subject, and the time and occasion are so right for the hearing, that every word will be fruitful of a deed. . . ."[9] Churchill is reported to have prepared with great care "because he very properly believed" that the Commoners had "a right to expect" his best.[10] Thus, your best should include five important characteristics:

1. Broad knowledge
2. Honest thinking
3. An urge to communicate
4. Recognition of your social responsibilities
5. A command of speaking techniques[11]

---

[7] Rosebery, quoted in Justice Birkett, "Churchill The Orator," in Charles Eade (Ed.), *Churchill*, Reprint Society, 1955, p. 227.

[8] Alfred Lord Tennyson, "Ulysses," in Jerome Hamilton Buckley (Ed.), *Poems of Tennyson*, Houghton Mifflin, 1958, pp. 66–67.

[9] Albert J. Beveridge, *The Art of Public Speaking*, Houghton Mifflin, 1924, pp. 19–20.

[10] Earl Winterton, quoted in Charles Eade (Ed.), *op. cit.*, pp. 48–58.

[11] For a complete discussion, see Giles Wilkeson Gray and Waldo W. Braden, *Public Speaking: Principles and Practice* (2nd ed.), Harper & Row, 1963, chap. 4.

Your Speaking Environment

The environment for a speech involves the time of the meeting, the assembly place, the prevailing customs of the locality, and the purpose of the meeting. You will find that the *where* and the *when* of a speech often have important bearings upon the outcome of your speaking effort. How do your remarks fit into the occasion? Why have you been asked to speak? What can you contribute to the occasion? For example, speaking at a noon luncheon meeting of a Kiwanis Club differs considerably from addressing a men's Sunday-school Bible class. The time and place make the difference. Think about these two cases. Gathering at noon, the business men must return to their establishments shortly after 1:00 P.M.; the length of the speech thus becomes most important. Now consider the Sunday-school members whose attitudes, interests, and activities center around the church, an affiliation making many subjects taboo.

The speaker must make his speaking consistent with social and political demands and any events which give rise to it.

Your Listeners

Franklin D. Roosevelt had the rare ability to personalize what he said, to give millions of radio listeners the warm feeling that he was talking directly to them. John Gunther said that F.D.R. "gave the impression, on the radio, of speaking to every listener personally, like a sympathetic, authoritative, and omniscient friend, . . . you could practically feel him physically in the room."[12] F.D.R. established *rapport,* the common feeling which binds speaker and listener together.

Take a lesson from Roosevelt: Never address an audience, but speak to individual listeners. The collective term *audience* is likely to imply an impersonal mass in which single faces are blurred and personal interests are forgotten. But in the act of assembling, listeners do not lose their identity, nor do they forget their personal aspirations and attitudes. As individuals, they have a warm glow for the speaker who shows his respect for each of them, who directs his

[12] John Gunther, *Roosevelt in Retrospect: A Profile in History,* Harper & Row, 1950, p. 38.

Fig. 1.5. F.D.R. was known "personally" by millions through his warm friendly radio voice. He had the rare ability to establish rapport with his individual listeners.

remarks to each, who seems eager to have each understand, and who appears to have a concern about the best interests of each.

When you face listeners, speak to individuals and respond to their facial reactions. Bonaro W. Overstreet—who, with her famous husband, is a popular lecturer and psychologist—has put this point well:

The wise lecturer [speaker] knows . . . that no matter how many hundred of people sit in front of him, lumped under the term *audience,* his words must reach each individual mind . . . or else go nowhere. He knows that if what he says . . . is to be worth the breath it takes, it must find its eventual lodging, not in the general atmosphere that hovers over the audience, but within the complex mental, emotional, and social structure of many different individual lives.[13]

[13] Bonaro W. Overstreet, "Speaking of Speakers," *Adult Leadership,* **I** (July–August, 1952), 3.

Thus, an effective speech is *listener centered*, a fact that requires you to direct your total effort toward reaching your listeners. Your foremost goal is to gain understanding, to arouse favorable attitudes, and to stir action. Harry Emerson Fosdick, the great Protestant preacher of our century, put "his emphasis on the audience, not only as the focal point of all preaching but also as influencing method in both composition and delivery."[14] Like Fosdick, put your ideas in the words and symbols of your listeners; develop your remarks at a rate commensurate with their understanding; conform always to what they consider good taste and acceptable behavior.

Your Speech

What is a speech? The question is not simple. Is an undelivered discourse in manuscript a speech? If a speaker reads an article aloud from *Reader's Digest*, is he delivering a speech? Is an impromptu recitation a speech? Does the auctioneer give a speech? Each of these trivial instances could be called a speech under the condition that *the speaker attempted to stir up meaning and to gain response from listeners.*

The genus *speech* may include a wide range of types: how-to-do-it talks, simple instructions, classroom lectures, political harangues, orations, addresses, and sermons. A few oral discourses such as those of Webster, Lincoln, and Churchill possess sufficient aesthetic excellence and universal appeal to be considered eloquent and to deserve places as great literature. But most speeches have a specific purpose to be satisfied at the immediate occasion. A speech may continue only a few seconds or several hours; it may be delivered on a street corner, at a boy scout camp-out, in a great hall, or in a legislature; it may be presented impromptu, extemporaneously, from memory, or from a manuscript. It may have any one of five purposes: to inform, to entertain, to stir enthusiasm, to gain acceptance of opinions, or to move to action.

James Winans once quipped that "a speech is not merely an essay standing on its hind legs."[15] G. W. Gray insists that a speech

[14] Roy C. McCall, "Harry Emerson Fosdick: A Study in Sources of Effectiveness," in Loren Reid (Ed.), *American Public Address*, Univ. of Missouri Press, 1961, p. 64.

[15] James Albert Winans and Hoyt Hopewell Hudson, *A First Course in Public Speaking*, Appleton-Century-Crofts, 1931, p. 17.

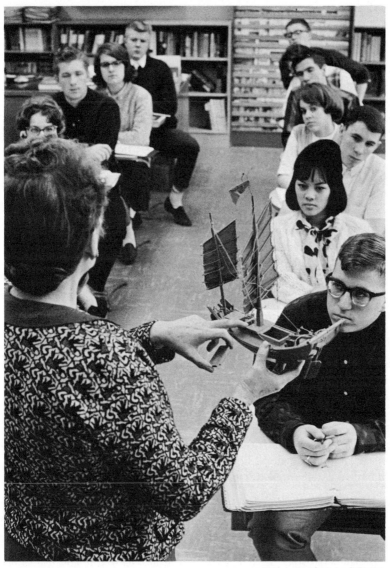

Fig. 1.6. A speech may have any of five purposes: to inform, to entertain, to stir enthusiasm, to gain acceptance of opinions, or to move to action.

does not consist of "language and delivery, but of delivered language."[16] In his view, a speech without an audience is not a speech; nor does a manuscript or printed speech embrace what occurs in the confrontation of speaker and listener. In his eulogy of Adams and Jefferson, Daniel Webster expresses much the same point of view when he characterizes great speaking: "It cannot be brought from far. Labor and learning may toil for it, but they will toil in vain. Words and phrases may be marshalled in every way, but they cannot compass it. It must exist in the man, in the subject and in the occasion."[17]

Speeches are utilitarian in purpose and method, and generally seek an immediate response from listeners.

Interaction of Elements of Speaking Situation

As we said, the speaking situation involves four *interacting* elements: (1) the speaker, (2) the environment, (3) the listeners, and (4) the speech. Spoken language becomes a speech only when there is *interaction* among these elements. Andrew Weaver explains that "speech is reciprocal in nature; the speaker stimulates the reactor, whose overt responses stimulate the speaker, who then restimulates the reactor, etc., etc., etc., so long as the speaking continues."[18] More recently this reciprocal process has been referred to as feedback.[19]

Let us illustrate how feedback works in practice. The alert speaker, sensing signs of misunderstanding, dismay, and disinterest immediately alters his presentation: He interrupts his development to insert an amusing story, becomes more enthusiastic, or solicits questions. He is delighted to have a vigorous and searching question; in

[16] Giles W. Gray, "Speech as an Academic Discipline," in Waldo W. Braden (Ed.) *Speech Methods and Resources*, Harper & Row, 1961, pp. 36–46.

[17] Daniel Webster, "Adams and Jefferson," in Edwin P. Whipple (Ed.), *The Great Speeches and Orations of Daniel Webster*, Little, Brown, 1899, p. 167.

[18] Andrew Weaver, "What Is Speech? A Symposium," *Quarterly Journal of Speech*, XLI (April, 1955), 145–153.

[19] For an amplified discussion see David K. Berlo, *The Process of Communication*, Holt, Rinehart and Winston, 1961, pp. 102–103.

Fig. 1.7. This speaker and his listeners are interacting. Here is a good illustration of feedback.

turn, he is stirred to give a forthright reply. By a change of pace, repartee, or humor, he stimulates other listeners to ask additional questions. The atmosphere has changed: Speaker and listeners pursue subject with fresh vigor.

Contrast this responsive speaker with the one who gives off signs of being subject-centered and is tied to his speech manuscript; he crams as much as possible into the time allotted to him. He does not tolerate questions or interruptions because he does not want to alter his organization, and he jealously guards each precious sentence and each example which he has so carefully and precisely phrased. If a listener dares bother him, he glares or makes a sarcastic retort. He will do nothing to change his prearranged plan. Because he seldom glances at his hearers, he misses their expressions of disgust, their nodding heads, and their newspaper reading.

Effective speeches are *listener-centered.* They are "delivered language."

QUESTIONS FOR INVESTIGATION AND DISCUSSION

1. What is the significance of Emerson's remark, "There is no true eloquence unless there is a man behind the speech"? What does he mean by *eloquence?* Does this advice apply to a student enrolled in a public-speaking class?
2. What are the four elements of the speaking situation? Are there other elements? In what way is this concept oversimplified?
3. What is the meaning of *interaction?* How does it take place? As a speaker, how can you ascertain when it is happening?
4. What are the differences between speaking to *listeners* and speaking to an *audience?* What are the characteristics of a speaker who speaks to an audience? To listeners?
5. What does Gray mean by "delivered language"?
6. What are implications of the phrase "speaking as one-way process"? As a "two-way process"? How are these phrases misleading?
7. What are some examples of feedback found in fields other than speech? Is the analogy to speaking sound?
8. What listener-rights does democratic society impose upon a speaker?
9. What is a *speech?* Look up several definitions. Also see Richard Murphy, "The Speech as Literary Genre," *Quarterly Journal of Speech,* XLIV (April, 1958), 117–127.
10. What are the characteristics of a speech that is "subject centered"? "Speaker centered"? "Listener centered"?
11. What are some other names for stage fright? What symptoms do you have? Why do you have these problems?

ASSIGNMENTS

SPEAKING ASSIGNMENTS

1. Deliver a two- to four-minute speech of introduction, following one of two approaches:

a. Introduce yourself, giving information that will help your classmate to know you.

b. Introduce another member of the class. (You may divide into
pairs or you may introduce the person seated on your right.)

2. Give a talk in which you tell about your previous speech
experiences: talks you have given, either directly to audiences or
over the air, meetings or clubs over which you have presided,
dramatic performances in which you have acted, different speaking
contests in which you have participated, groups in which you have
served as counselor or instructor, courses you have taken. What
texts have you studied, and who were your instructors?

RESEARCH ASSIGNMENT

Prepare a report on one of the articles given in Suggested Readings.

BULLETIN-BOARD ASSIGNMENT

If you have a bulletin board in your classroom, someone in your
class should be responsible each week for mounting materials on a
chosen subject. You may contribute pictures, cartoons, or articles
which you find pertinent to the topic of the week. If you can
draw, perhaps you will want to do some cartoons. When you come
to class, spend a few minutes studying what has been posted. Be
sure to give the source, i.e., newspaper, page, date. Also put your
name on the clipping so that other members of the class will know
who has been responsible.

Theme: "Public Speaking Is Important."

SUGGESTED READINGS

Baird, A. Craig, "Responsibilities of Free Communication," *Vital
Speeches of the Day,* **18** (September 1, 1952), 699–701.
Braden, Waldo W., "Speech, Science, and the Future," *Speech
Teacher,* **X** (September, 1961), 184–188.
Brigance, William Norwood, "Demagogues, 'Good' People, and

Teachers of Speech," *Speech Teacher,* **I** (September, 1952), 157–162.

Carleton, William G., "Effective Speech in a Democracy," *Vital Speeches of the Day,* **17** (June 15, 1951), 540–544.

Gray, Giles Wilkeson, and Waldo W. Braden, *Public Speaking: Principles and Practice* (2nd ed.), Harper & Row, 1963, chaps. 1 and 4.

Harrington, Elbert W., "The Role of Speech in Liberal Education," *Quarterly Journal of Speech,* **XLI** (October, 1955), 219–222.

Klotsche, J. Martin, "The Importance of Communication in Today's World," *Speech Teacher,* **XI** (November, 1962), 322–326.

Nilsen, Thomas R., "Free Speech, Persuasion, and the Democratic Process," *Quarterly Journal of Speech,* **XLIV** (October, 1958), 235–243.

Oliver, Robert T., "Culture and Communication," *Vital Speeches of the Day,* **29** (September 15, 1963), 721–724.

Oliver, Robert T., "Speech and the Community," *Vital Speeches of the Day,* **29** (May 15, 1963), 459–462.

II

RESOURCES FOR SUBJECTS AND MATERIALS

Success comes to the speaker who chooses his subjects wisely—topics that seem to fit the speaking environment uniquely and to stir the attention and interest of listeners. The mediocre speaker complains that he has nothing worthwhile to say, and that it has been his misfortune to have lived in a locality where little exciting ever happens. What he says may be true, but usually a little investigation will show that the fault is not "in his stars" but in himself; he has really never taken a hard look around to seek out promising subjects.

But stir up the novice, challenge his very existence, demand that he defend what is precious and sacred to him, and you will discover that even a mundane person suddenly approaches eloquence. For example, a little Cajun girl, when forced to defend her little community in French Louisiana, spoke fervently and fluently. The author has encountered numerous similar instances. Here are a few that he remembers from the hundreds of speeches he has heard:

A Mississippi boy telling about his reaction to a snake bite
A college freshmen recounting how he killed his first deer·
A former pilot attempting to explain what it meant to stay over a target in North Korea for just 60 seconds
An insurance adjuster arguing for highway safety
An 18-year-old freshman coed challenging G. I. attitudes

None of these persons was a great speaker, but each had discovered the importance of the urge to communicate; each intensified his speaking through concentration on what he was particularly well informed about and in what he believed.

SOURCES OF TOPICS AND MATERIALS

As a starting point in laying your plans to become an effective speaker, you need to learn how to marshal your speech materials. How well you do your home work will have much to do with your speaking success. Successful speakers seem to have an inexhaustible source of good speech subjects and supporting materials. But they will be the first to tell you about how much time goes into their reading and searching. Heed their advice and become a searcher and hoarder! Below are several places to start your search.

1. Take a Look at Yourself

Start your search for subjects and materials by taking an inventory of where you have been, what you are, and what you are uniquely qualified to speak about. You are an authority on at least one subject —yourself. On what topics have you information that no one else can duplicate? Don't be modest! Be specific! If at first you can think of nothing, stir yourself up.

Fig. 2.1. Informal spontaneous "eloquence" at an unexpected moment.

2. *Examine Your Own Convictions*

Most persons have strong feelings, attitudes, sentiments, or opinions on several issues or problems. In what do you believe? Are you a Republican, a Democrat, a States Righter, a Conservative, or a Liberal? Do you favor or oppose fraternities, social clubs, country clubs, or business-men luncheon clubs? How do you stand on integration or segregation? Are you religious? Some of these and similar questions should open up many subjects.

3. *Study Your Prospective Listeners*

Your listeners probably have beliefs and opinions which are equally as intense and important to them as yours are to you. Seek out these areas. As a starting place, check their average age, economic status, religious affiliations, social activities, peculiar associations, and responsibilities. Search for fields in which many of them have common ties.

4. Analyze the Speaking Occasion

Why have you been asked to speak at this time? Do the time and place suggest topics? If you are a keynote speaker at a conference, you will want to study what happens on such occasions, and why. Labor Day, Flag Day, the Fourth of July, Washington's birthday, Lincoln's birthday, D-day, and commencements provide thousands of speakers with challenging opportunities to give vent to their feelings.

5. Note the Speeches of Prominent Persons

When you hear a business leader, a political figure, a prominent scholar, or a great preacher, listen for usable topics and ideas. Look for new slants to old questions; jot down ideas which a speaker may suggest for further exploration. Do not limit your search only to what you hear; make a habit of reading *Vital Speeches of the Day, Representative American Speeches* (H. W. Wilson Co.), *The New York Times,* and the *Congressional Record.* Don't overlook collections of great speeches of the past—*Modern Eloquence,* for example. Such sources should provide a long list of subjects and a stack of materials.

6. Search Editorial Pages and Syndicated Columns

A Walter Lippmann, an Arthur Krock, a James Reston, or a David Lawrence may provide many valuable leads and stimulating commentaries. William S. White reports that the U.S. senators look to such figures with considerable respect: "Many men in the Senate . . . would rather have an approving reference by a Krock or a Lippmann than a full laudatory column in the hometown paper."[1] What is important to a senator should provide at least a hint to you. The editorial opinions expressed in distinguished papers such as *The New York Times,* the *St. Louis Post Dispatch,* the *Christian Science Monitor,* or the *Wall Street Journal* often contain germs of ideas for speeches. They also provide many excellent examples.

[1] William S. White, *Citadel: The Story of the U.S. Senate,* Harper & Row, 1957, pp. 167–168.

7. Be Alert to Print and Broadcast Material

Newspapers, news magazines, radio, and television continue to pour forth voluminous materials. Pay particular attention to feature articles. You should push your horizon beyond the local press and regional broadcasting stations.

You will also find the news magazines and better periodicals full of good speech materials: Make it a habit to look through such magazines as the *Atlantic, Harper's, Fortune, New Republic, The Nation, Newsweek, The Reporter, Time,* and *U. S. News and World Report.* Articles in these can be located through *Readers' Guide to Periodical Literature.* Don't overlook *The New York Times Magazine,* a section in the Sunday edition, and the magazine sections in other Sunday papers.

8. See What Government Publications Are Available

The Government Printing Office is continually issuing informative publications on numerous subjects. You can keep abreast of current materials by requesting that your name be placed on the mailing list for a free leaflet entitled *Selected United States Government Publications.*[2] The reports of bureaus, departments, and congressional committees also assemble many facts and opinions. Also consult the *Congressional Record,* including its Appendix. Ask your local librarian to help you locate the materials. Also, a letter to your Congressman will generally bring you a prompt response with materials.

9. Seek Materials from Professional and Business Organizations

The best index to this type of material is *The Vertical File Service Catalog,* which gives title, author, publisher, and price, and lists many free and little-known publications. But do not be discouraged if your library does not have this index, for numerous leaflets and booklets are readily available. If you are interested in safety, for example, call a local industry to inquire what it can supply. A local chamber of commerce, a philanthropic group, a public-health agency, civic clubs, insurance companies, and agencies of the local,

[2] Write Superintendent of Documents, Government Printing Office, Washington 25, D.C.

Fig. 2.2. Conversation among friends often serves to release creative thinking and to develop new insights.

state, and national governments may have great quantities of printed information available for the asking. Furthermore, letters to the national offices of various pressure groups and private foundations will usually bring additional leaflets and pamphlets. For up-to-date lists of addresses, see the latest edition of the *World Almanac,* under the title "Organizations, Clubs."

10. Use Your Friends and Associates as Sources

"Conversation is the oldest form of instruction of the human race." It is still "an indispensable one," says A. Whitney Griswold, former president of Yale University. He further calls it "the hand-maid of learning, true religion, and free government."[3]

Of course, not all friends will give you "instruction," particularly when they limit their chatter to bridge hands, diet, football, sport cars, movies, or sex. But with well-informed and vigorous associates,

[3] A. Whitney Griswold, "This Tongue-tied Democracy: On Conversation, Chiefly Academic," *Vital Speeches of the Day,* **21** (November 1, 1954), 828–832.

conversation can bring new insights and serve as a release to creative thinking. Alfred North Whitehead once said that "outside of book-knowledge," he got most of his development from "the good conversation."[4] Seemingly others have found the same; great minds stimulate other great minds and, through mutual interchange, they enliven each other.

11. Don't Overlook the Great Books

It may not always be possible to have a conversation with a great man, but you can always reach the thinking of great men through your reading. The wide variety of available paperbacks put the best at your disposal at small cost. Bacon, of course, had a point when he said, "Some books are to be tasted, others to be swallowed, and some few to be chewed and digested."[5] In the same vein, Benjamin Franklin once said, "Reading makes a full man—meditation a profound man—discourse a clear man."[6] As you do with your friends, choose your books with care, but it makes no difference whether they are classics or contemporary. Sometimes you may find excellent materials in unexpected places.

12. Try Brainstorming

The birth of an original idea is often a painful process. Too often you cannot open up your creative side because you have channelled your thinking along established lines. The first 11 suggestions of this section should start you on the way, but they may not move you to force yourself out of the habitual patterns of thought and analysis. You need an additional push. You need to strain and stretch yourself, looking for new orientations and different slants to old problems.

Try the following scheme: Set yourself the goal of writing 100 or more topics in a limited time. As long as you find it easy to add to the list, you have not reached the crucial test. Only when you must agonize and grope are you likely to become inventive. In preparing

---

[4] *Ibid.*

[5] Francis Bacon, "Of Studies," *Selected Writing of Francis Bacon,* Random House, 1955, p. 199.

[6] Benjamin Franklin, "Poor Richard, 1738," Leonard W. Larabee (Ed.), *The Papers of Benjamin Franklin,* Yale Univ. Press, 1960, vol. 2, p. 196.

such an inventory, it may be a good idea to group your topics under two headings: informative and persuasive (see the Table of Speech Subjects). Add to your list whenever a new topic occurs to you. Carry a pad and pencil in order to take advantage of unexpected flashes and inspiration whenever they strike.

TABLE OF SPEECH SUBJECTS

Speeches to Inform	Speeches to Convince and to Actuate
1. Criticism	1. Political problems
a. Movies	a. International
b. Plays	b. Regional
c. Speeches	c. National
d. Literature	d. Sectional
2. Current events	e. State
3. Definitions	f. County
4. Descriptions	g. Local
5. Explanations and demonstrations	h. Personal
a. Apparatus	2. Agricultural problems
b. Machines	3. Industrial problems
c. Tools	4. Business problems
d. Processes	5. Labor problems
e. Procedures	6. Educational problems
6. Reviews	7. Family problems
a. Books	8. Religious problems
b. Plays	9. Philosophical and ethical problems
c. Movies	10. Social problems
7. Interpretations	11. Scientific problems
a. Social customs and mores	12. Personal affairs
b. Religion	
c. Political affairs	
d. Government	
e. History	
8. Travelogues	

SOURCE: Adapted from Giles Wilkeson Gray and Waldo W. Braden, *Public Speaking: Principles and Practice* (2nd ed.), Harper & Row, 1963, p. 210.

CHECKING THE SUITABILITY OF A SPEECH SUBJECT

Popular manuals advise that you talk about subjects "closest to your heart." But wait, isn't there another element to be considered? The greatest bores on earth are those incessant talkers who go on endlessly about what is "closest" to their hearts; in fact, they carry their enthusiasms so far that they will not let anyone else talk. We run when we see them coming; we make fun of them. Remember the speech is to be *listener centered*—not *speaker centered*. Before you select a subject, ask yourself whether it will fit the speaking environment and whether you can make it listener-centered.

Consider five important questions:

1. Does the subject provide something which is important to my listeners?
2. Do I have, or can I find, enough information to make this subject worth the time of my listeners?
3. Do I have an urge to communicate this subject to my listeners?
4. Is the subject consistent with the requirements of the occasion?
5. Can I develop the subject adequately within the time limit?

A "yes" answer to each of the five questions means that you are ready to move forward in your preparation.

BUILDING A BACKGROUND

The title of this section poses a difficult task for the student who attempts to satisfy its demand in a weekend. More properly, it is the goal of liberal education which strives to provide a rich context for living. Great speakers are often avid readers. They spend weeks and even months preparing their speeches. They do not produce their masterful orations overnight. Emerson has said, "One must be an inventor to read well. As the proverb says, 'He that would bring

Fig. 2.3. Make sure that your speech topic is *listener centered.*

home the wealth of the Indies must carry out the wealth of the Indies.' "[7]

However, knowing your library and its resources is a necessary first step in your search for materials. Below are several books and magazines that bring together articles on current topics:

The Reference Shelf Series (H. W. Wilson Co.). Each volume encompasses articles and addresses on a current subject.

The Forensic Quarterly, edited by Charley Leistner as service to

---

[7] Ralph Waldo Emerson, "The American Scholar," in Wayland Maxfield Parrish and Marie Hochmuth (Eds.), *American Speeches,* McKay, 1954, pp. 264–283.

Fig. 2.4. To become thoroughly familiar with your library and its resources helps in acquiring and assimilating the materials for your speech.

high school debaters, contains articles on the current high-school debate proposition.

The Annals of the American Academy of Political and Social Science, a bimonthly scholarly journal, is devoted to controversial subjects involving the foreign policy, domestic problems, and religion.

The Congressional Digest, not a government publication, which devotes each issue to a single controversial subject, giving articles, pro and con. It is not to be confused with the *Congressional Record,* which contains the proceedings of the U.S. Senate and House of Representatives.

The World Almanac, the *Information Please Almanac,* the *Britannica Book of the Year,* the *Americana Annual,* the *Census Reports, The Statistical Abstract of the U.S.* present much statistical and factual information.

DEVELOPING A SPEECH-MATERIALS FILE

Locating materials is not enough; you must have a systematic way to file away provocative articles, humorous stories, fresh examples, well-phrased ideas, pithy sayings, and striking phraseology. Also, when you start actual preparation, you must be able to find what is pertinent. Norman Vincent Peale, dynamic New York preacher, uses the following method:

He would choose topics for several weeks ahead, assemble provocative titles to go with those topics, and then mark the titles on cardboard folders into which he would drop newspaper clippings, apt quotations, and memoranda to himself about stories or anecdotes that might serve as illustrations of the main point.[8]

Among the private papers of Franklin D. Roosevelt, deposited at Hyde Park, are his "Speech Materials Files." These collections of miscellany give considerable insight into the research that went into Roosevelt's speeches. For example, a folder on a given subject may include such items as the following:

Memoranda from numerous persons
Letters, private and open
Newspaper and magazine clippings
Press releases
Statistical reports
Excerpts from the *Congressional Record*
Printed copies of Supreme Court decisions
Reports of meetings of national groups
Stories and anecdotes from letters, clippings, etc.
Apt phrases from speeches and writings of important personages

[8] Arthur Gordon, *Norman Vincent Peale, Minister to Millions,* Prentice-Hall, 1958, pp. 179–180.

Fig. 2.5. A speech-materials file of your own is a valuable asset in preparing for a speech. Keep up to date with the print media—particularly the editorial pages and syndicated columns—and make a durable clipping file of all that you deem pertinent.

including St. Thomas Aquinas, Erasmus, Francis Bacon, Gouverneur Morris, George Washington, Alexander Hamilton, Thomas Jefferson, Abraham Lincoln, etc.

It will be to your advantage to adopt some kind of systematic filing system: manila folders, large 9″ × 12″ envelopes, a scrapbook, or a card file. If you use 5″ × 8″ cards, you may paste newspaper articles to them, or perhaps glue or staple to the card a small-size letter envelope into which you may insert clippings.

Label each item carefully, giving the source, the date, and the page number. In note-taking, use a uniform system of labeling and

Gross National Product

"As fresh evidence of the nation's economic
vigor accumulated last week, President
Johnson reported that the gross national
product, the dollar measure of the
economy's entire output, climbed by $9.7
billion in the second quarter of 1964 to a
record annual rate of $618.5 billion."

Newsweek, 64:58 July 27, 1964

Propaganda, definition

"Propaganda [is] the dissemination of
conclusions from concealed sources or with
concealed objectives. This process short-
cuts reflection and thought, utilizes
selection and distortion, in place of
more impartial education, and involves an
element of deviousness."

William Albig, Modern Public
Opinion, McGraw-Hill, 1956,
p. 302.

Standard of living

It is "scale of consumption of an individual, group, or nation considered in
relation to its socio-economic status.
. . . The items which make up a standard
of living include not only the material
articles of consumption, but also the
number of dependents in a family, the
environment, the educational facilities,
and the amount spent for health,
recreation and social services."

The Columbia Encyclopedia,
Third edition (1963), p. 2030.

employ standard rules for recording material. The following 10 suggestions will prove helpful:

1. Label clearly and uniformly.
2. Write clearly, and do not crowd material.
3. Do not put more than one subject on a card.
4. Do not distort meaning by lifting material out of context.
5. If you copy verbatim, enclose in quotation marks. (For a quotation within a quotation, use single quotes.)
6. Delete unnecessary portions and indicate by using three dots (. . .) for deletion within a sentence and four dots (. . . .) for deletions at end of sentence.
7. Quote exactly. If the material seems in error, if words are omitted, or if words are misspelled, place [sic] immediately following the discrepancy to indicate that the mistake or deletion has been noted.
8. To indicate interpolation within a quotation, place remark within brackets, not parentheses.
9. Indicate italicized words by underlining.
10. After copying material, check it against original before proceeding.

Please note in Fig. 2.6 that on each card a clear label is placed in upper left-hand corner, that quotation marks are included, and that source is given. Be sure to indicate when material is deleted (see third example) and when words are added (see second example).

QUESTIONS FOR INVESTIGATION AND DISCUSSION

1. What are some places where you can look for speech subjects and materials? Are there some sources not mentioned in this chapter?

Fig. 2.6.   Some examples of note cards. Clear topical labels are put at the upper left hand corner to facilitate alphabetical or other systematic filing and locating.   *Top:* From a magazine   *Middle:* From a book *Bottom:* From an encyclopedia

2. What does Emerson mean by the statement that a reader "must be an inventor"? You may want to read "The American Scholar," in Wayland Maxfield Parrish and Marie Hochmuth (Eds.), *American Speeches*, McKay, 1954, pp. 264–283.

3. What does Emerson imply when he says in "The American Scholar," "Meek young men grow up in libraries, believing it their duty to accept the views which Cicero, which Locke, which Bacon, have given; forgetful that Cicero, Locke, and Bacon were only young men in libraries when they wrote these books." This quotation could be made the subject of a speech.

4. What great books are a fruitful source of speech material? How must you be an "inventor" to use such materials?

5. How do prominent speakers collect materials for their speeches (see source materials)?

6. What types of speech materials can you find in the newspapers? Prepare a list of columns or sections of a given paper which might provide materials. For example, see the columns on the editorial page of the *Wall Street Journal* entitled "Notable & Quotable," and see "Mirror of World Opinion" in the *Christian Science Monitor*.

7. What resources does your local library hold for the speaker? Newspapers? Reference works? Collections of speeches? Books of quotations?

8. What are considered the best newspapers in the United States? How many of these are available to you locally?

9. What local agencies may have pamphlet materials which you could get for speech materials?

10. What pressure groups and private foundations may supply you with materials? Make a list of at least 10 which you might consult.

ASSIGNMENTS

RESEARCH ASSIGNMENTS

1. Cooperative project in learning about the availability of speech materials in your local library. Prepare a five-minute report on the

usefulness of one of the following items as a source of speech materials:

The Annals of the American Academy of Political and Social Science
Bartlett's Familiar Quotations, or any similar book
Congressional Digest
A Dictionary of Contemporary American Usage, by Bergen Evans and Cornelia Evans
The Oxford Companion to American Literature
The Oxford Companion to English Literature
Information Please Almanac
The Reference Shelf Series
The Statesman's Year Book
The World Almanac
Statistical Abstract
The Economic Almanac
Editorial Research Reports
Any annual volume of an encyclopedia
An item of your own choice

2. On the basis of the speeches of introduction, prepare a list of areas in which your classmates are interested.

3. Prepare a list of one hundred speech topics which you think would be appropriate for class talks. Study carefully the "Sources of Speech Subjects" found on page 32. You may wish to record your list under two headings: informative speeches and persuasive speeches. Be as specific as possible.

4. Prepare a five-minute report on one of the articles listed under Suggested Readings.

BULLETIN BOARD ASSIGNMENT

Theme: Illustrations of Speech Materials.

SUGGESTED READINGS

Adler, Mortimer J., *How to Read a Book: The Art of Getting a Liberal Education,* Simon and Schuster, 1940.

Aldrich, Ella Virginia, *Using Books and Libraries* (4th ed.), Prentice-Hall, 1960.

Goheen, Robert F., "The Liberal Arts," *Vital Speeches of the Day*, **29** (March 1, 1963), 318–320.

Gray, Giles Wilkeson, and Waldo W. Braden, *Public Speaking: Principles and Practice* (2nd ed.), Harper & Row, 1963, chap. 12.

Griswold, A. Whitney, "This Tongue-Tied Democracy: On Conversation—Chiefly Academic," *Vital Speeches of the Day*, **21** (November 1, 1954), 828–832.

Harding, Harold F., "What Are Your Ultimate Objectives?" *Vital Speeches of the Day*, **29** (October 1, 1963), 757–760.

Lennon, E. James, "More Effective Illustrations of Speech Techniques," *Speech Teacher*, **II** (January, 1953), 52–54.

McBath James H. (Ed.), *Argumentation and Debate: Principles and Practices* (rev. ed.), Holt, Rinehart and Winston, 1963, chap. 5.

Miller, Melvin H., "When Found Make a Note Of," *Today's Speech*, **X** (September, 1962), 10–11.

O'Brien, Harold J., "How To Think Creatively," *Today's Speech*, **V** (November, 1957), 17–19.

Walter, Otis M., "Creativity: A Neglected Factor in Public Speaking," *Speech Teacher*, **III** (September, 1954), 159–168.

White, Eugene E., *Practical Public Speaking* (2nd ed.), Macmillan, 1964, chap. 4.

Winchell, Constance M., *Guide to Reference Books* (7th ed.), American Library Association, 1951.

III

HOW TO ORGANIZE
A SPEECH

Remember that a speech is not an essay. To achieve its purpose, a speech must be almost instantly intelligible. If, at the moment of utterance, the listener chooses not to listen, if he cannot hear, if the language is not clear, or if the sequence of ideas is not apparent, oral effort is likely to fail. Now contrast the speech with printed discourse. If, upon a first reading, the reader fails to comprehend the message, he simply stops, turns back, and rereads. He may look up unfamiliar words; he may meditate at length about a word or a given passage; he may discuss it with a friend; he may consult

Fig. 3.1. Television presentations require excellent oral organization. This speaker's composure and cordial friendliness immediately reassure her listeners.

other works on the subject; he may reread difficult passages aloud. He may reread a second or third time to seek out rich connotative implications. In fact, good writing packs in rich shades of meaning which become apparent with reflection. Further, it is so carefully constructed that the sequence of ideas flow smoothly into each other without the structure being too apparent.

Speaking is a continuous, ever flowing process as long as the speaker continues to put out sound waves. There is no way to stop these waves, to rewind and play them again. Of course, it is possible on occasion to ask questions for clarification and amplification, but even then the speaker utters each sentence only once, and repeating an obtuse statement may not stir up any additional meaning. Once the speaker encodes his message into oral language and utters it, he has completed his part in the communication cycle; the meaning that is stirred up depends almost entirely upon the decoding of the listener.

How can a speaker ensure greater effectiveness of the oral process? At least one important way to help the listener is through *oral organization;* that is, the type of unfolding which keeps the listener informed as to where the speaker is at frequent intervals. It involves repeating points for emphasis and stressing the sequence, interrelationships, and succession of points and subpoints.

PRINCIPLES OF ORAL ORGANIZATION

First, oral organization makes effective use of repetition. In some speeches it is advisable to repeat each main point as many as *four times.* For example:

Preview main points to be developed
State, develop, and restate each main point
Review all main points

Second, oral organization makes use of sign posts, or point indicators. Each main point is clearly labeled with a "first," "second," or "third," or some other device which calls a new point to the attention of the listener. For example:

My first point is. . . .
My second point is. . . .
My third point is. . . .

Third, oral organization takes into the consideration the difficulties of comprehension and retention of oral material; consequently, it employs such devices as:

1. Wording points in short declarative sentences, 10 words or less if possible
2. Wording main points in parallel form
3. Limiting main points to not more than five; preferably three or less
4. Using internal summaries when development is involved

5. Including visual aids to keep points before audience—strip charts, flannel boards, etc.

6. Including thought breaks and opportunities to ask questions

Oral organization is made as obvious to the listener as possible. You tell your listeners again and again in order to get through, stirring up the meanings which you intend. You keep the development as simple as possible.

THE INFORMATIVE SPEECH

Determining and Arranging Points

Assuming that you understand oral organization, now let us turn to the steps of putting an informative speech together.

First, determine your central thought or subject sentence. What is your talk about? Boil your ideas down into a single, short, simple sentence which states what you want your listeners to comprehend. You may phrase it in one of the following forms:

1. A one-sentence definition to be developed
2. A question to be answered
3. A sentence which partitions your subject

Second, select the main points to develop your central thought (see p. 45 for form and suggestions).

Third, determine and arrange the supporting points. You may accomplish this step by employing any one of the following methods:[1]

1. *According to chronological or time order.* This sequence moves from the past to future or in reverse:

> In 1850 we. . . .
> In 1900 we. . . .
> In 1950 we. . . .

2. *According to a space or physical layout.* This sequence involves ordering the points according to structure or contiguity; that is,

[1] The categories given are not intended to be mutually exclusive; some overlap.

Fig. 3.2. The informative speech should be clearly organized according to major and subordinate facts and should proceed in a logical sequence. Supporting materials, such as illustrations, graphics, and other aids should be on hand in the same order as your speech plan.

how the parts fit together—right to left, top to bottom, corner to corner, inside—outside, east to west, far to near, and the opposite of each of these:

At the top of the map. . . .
In the middle of the map. . . .
At the bottom of the map. . . .

3. *According to operations.* Operational order is similar to chronological order in that the steps or points follow a product
through a machine or the unfolding of a process or procedure:

> The first step is crushing.
> The second step is clarification.
> The third step is concentration.
> The fourth step is crystallization.

4. *According to development.* Like that just described, this sequence is essentially a time order in that it follows growth,
emergence, or evolution. It moves from inception onward or the
reverse:

> The company was created by. . . .
> The company incorporated in. . . .
> The company was merged with. . . .
> The company was expanded when. . . .

5. *According to the parties involved.* This scheme orders the points
according to types, classes, persons participating in an activity,
etc.:

> The freshmen. . . .
> The sophomores. . . .
> The juniors. . . .
> The seniors. . . .

6. *According to fields of endeavor.* This arrangement considers the
aspects, realms, or the scope of a subject:

> From the social. . . .
> From the religious. . . .
> From the political. . . .
> From the economic. . . .

7. *According to component parts.* This organization divides the
speech into a discussion of way a machine or organization is put
together:

> The wheels. . . .
> The frame. . . .
> The body. . . .

Fig. 3.3. The first item in any speech plan should be geared to gain the listeners' *attention.*

8. *According to cause and effect.* Under this scheme, the points fall under the headings of cause and effect:

> The cause is. . . .
> The results are three: . . .

Fourth, commit the outline to written form:

I. How I intend to get an attentive hearing.
II. How I intend to relate subject to interests and wants (motives) of listeners.
III. Central thought: . . . .
    Point A: . . . .
          1. . . . .
          2. . . . .
    Point B: . . . .
          1. . . . .
          2. . . . .

    Point C: . . . .
            1. . . . .
            2. . . . .
IV. Summary:
    A. . . . .
    B. . . . .
    C. . . . .

Formula for Presenting an Entire Speech

The *short, one-point speech* may not require extensive development. It may be presented as follows:

1. *Opening.* In not more than two or three sentences tell listeners why it is important to listen to you. *Hit a sensitive nerve,* or "build a fire."
2. *State your main central thought.* Remember only one short (10 words or less) sentence.
3. *Make the point clear.* You may use narration, description, exposition, examples, and visual aids.
4. *Conclusion.* Restate the central thought in the same sentence used in 2, above.

For *the longer speech,* the plan given for the single-point talk is easily expanded:

1. *Introduction.* Focus interest on subject by one of the following means:

> Arouse curiosity as to what is coming
> Make a startling statement
> Tell an amusing or exciting story
> Hit a sensitive nerve by working on motives

2. State the central thought.
3. Preview main points to be developed.
4. Develop body of speech. For each point:

> State
> Develop
> Restate

5. *Conclusion.* Review points developed.

The following "thumbnail sketch" illustrates this type of development in more expanded form, using as the speech topic "How to Select a Nail":

THUMBNAIL SKETCH OF AN INFORMATIVE TALK

How to Select a Nail

INTRODUCTION

Hit a sensitive nerve: Knowing your nails may save you hours and effort when you do home repair.

Central thought: There are four basic types of nails.

Preview: In this talk, I plan to tell you about first, a wire nail; second, a box nail; third, a finishing nail; and fourth, a casing nail. Let me write the four key words on the chalkboard.

DEVELOPMENT

First, have a look at the common wire nail. It is the rough, tough member of the family, built for heavy work. For example, you would use it to nail a board on the garden gate or to fasten down a loose board on a cellar step.

Second, here is its slender cousin, the box nail. This thinner nail is useful where a common nail might split the board. For example, you could nail together two apple boxes with one of these.

Third, notice that the finishing nail has a shapely head that can be set below the surface of the wood. For example, you could use this fellow to fasten down a piece of loose siding on your house.

Fourth, a casing nail is used for interior trim. For example, this type serves to fasten interior trim—like the molding that runs around the walls just below the ceiling.

CONCLUSION

Don't let them forget: Select the best nail for the right job. Never let it be said that you don't know your nails. Remember these four types which I have written on the chalkboard: the common wire nail, the box nail, the finishing nail, and the casing nail.

Fig. 3.4. This speaker's forceful delivery stirs up a favorable reaction from his listeners.

THE PERSUASIVE SPEECH

The informative speech attempts to make clear, to impart understanding and to encourage retention. In contrast, the persuasive speech has as its goal to stir up favorable attitudes, to change opinions, and to elicit action (see Chapter X for full development). The organization required to achieve these three goals are indeed different from those in the informative talk.

Determine What You Want of Your Listeners

Write your thought into a *one-sentence proposition* which either asserts a thought or recommends a course of action.

The proposition should meet the following requirements: (1) a short simple declarative sentence; (2) worded in language of the listeners and easy to remember; and (3) using the verb in the active voice.

Assertive propositions:
> The intrusion of salt water threatens the water supply.
> The Red Cross needs our support.
> Drinking and driving do not mix.

Recommending propositions:
> You should buy a new car.
> State University should install parking meters.
> Valley City should purchase the city bus system.
> The University should prohibit freshmen from bringing cars on the campus.

Proving the Assertive Proposition

This type of proposition, sometimes referred to as a proposition of fact, affirms or denies the existence of a fact, a truth, a condition, an influence, or a relationship. It asks the listener for a change of his opinion or belief.

When you hear this type of proposition, you should ask a *why* question. If the speaker asserts, "Crawford College needs your financial support," you should want to know, "Why does Crawford College need my support?" or "What reasons are there for me to support Crawford College?"

Let us look for some reasons to support this proposition:

Crawford College needs our support, because
1. Present income is insufficient to meet current expenses.
2. The college needs funds to construct a new library.
3. The college needs funds to increase the faculty salaries.

U. S. Public Health Service

Fig. 3.5. Clear partitioning of points on posters and feltboards will assist your listeners in more easily remembering the high points of your talk.

Notice that each point is a reason for agreeing with the statement that the college "needs support." The inclusion of the word *because* emphasizes this close logical relationship.

Below is an outline for a persuasive speech which illustrates this development:

Speech Outline

Seat Belts

INTRODUCTION

Cornell University researches estimate that if large numbers of automobile drivers would use seat belts, 5,000 lives could be saved each year.

Proposition: Seat belts save lives.

DEVELOPMENT

I. They prevent the occupant from being ejected in case of accident.

A. Car occupants are as much as 60% safer inside the case in case of an accident.
B. The risk of death is five times greater for those thrown from car.
II. They reduce impact with interior surfaces.
 A. This factor may mean difference between minor and major injury.
 B. This factor may prevent being thrown against windshield.
III. They keep driver from being wrenched from control of wheel.
 A. Driver has better control of car during and after impact.
 B. Driver can prevent additional damage.

CONCLUSION

The American Medical Association and National Safety Council agree that the seat belt is the best self-help available to cut the toll of dead and injured—if an accident does happen.

Formulas for the Persuasive Speech

In a popular little book entitled, *Public Speaking: As Listeners Like It* (Harper & Row, 1935), Richard C. Borden has summarized effective organization in the following four short sentences:

> Ho hum!
> Why bring that up!
> For instance.
> So what!

Borden says that "ho hum," means "kindle a quick flame of spontaneous interest."

"Why bring that up" involves "building a bridge" to an island of the listener's interests.

"For instance" (or "get down to cases"), refers to giving "some purposeful general assertions about your subject."

By "so what!" he means asking for action.

Borden's suggestion is a good scheme for the persuasive speaker. To stir action, the speaker must:

1. Gain and hold interest
2. Create a desire
3. Offer a method of satisfying the desire
4. Appeal for acceptance and action

This formula involves the following five steps:

1. Introduction
2. Problem
3. Solution
4. Advantage
5. Appeal for action

Alan Monroe dramatized these steps by presenting them as a motivated sequence:

1. The attention step
2. The need step
3. The satisfaction step
4. The visualization step
5. The action step[2]

The introduction attempts to gain a favorable hearing for the speaker, and, of course, attempts to focus attention on the problem, to establish the right of the speaker to talk on the subject, and to clarify any confusing or unfamiliar terms in the proposition.

The problem, or need step, tells the listener why he should be concerned about difficulty at hand. It may consider the causes of the problem as well as its manifestations. It may point out how the inherent weaknesses result in serious consequences for the listener.

The solution, or plan of action, is usually stated or implied in the proposition; e.g., "give to Crawford College"; "buy a new car"; "oppose integration"; "join the church." This step gives the listener a way to alleviate the difficulties with which he finds himself involved.

The advantages, or visualization step, pictures how the situation would be if the proposal has been put into operation.

The appeal-for-action step attempts to push the listener into acceptance and action; it involves bringing as much pressure as possible upon the listener to act.

The following "Thumbnail Sketch" illustrates in detail the formula of a persuasive speech:

[2] Alan Monroe, *Principles and Types of Speech* (5th ed.), Scott, Foresman, 1962, pp. 280–302.

Thumbnail Sketch of a Persuasive Speech

Seat Belts

INTRODUCTION

Build a fire: Will you be found dead with your seat belt unfastened: What a tragedy! Buckle up and live. The life you save could be your own.

DEVELOPMENT

Problem: Every year almost 40,000 lives are lost in traffic accidents. Three out of four traffic deaths occur within 25 miles of home. You could be in one of these accidents. How lucky you are that you have not been injured or even killed.

Solution: If it should happen, would you like to improve your chances of survival in the accident? If you do, install and use seat belts. They will cost you about twenty-five dollars, less than a season ticket to L.S.U. football games.

Advantage: The National Safety Council says that with a seat belt fastened you are 35 to 60% safer than you are without one.

CONCLUSION

Appeal for Action: Why risk death or critical injury! Be safe! Install those seat belts today and then use them. Join the thousands of Americans who protect themselves and their families with seat belts.

IMPORTANT PRINCIPLES OF OUTLINING

Outlining is an important part of your speech preparation. Take time to put the parts of the speech together carefully. Through this process of analysis and synthesis you can check the soundness of your thinking, ensure the coherence of your ideas, and move toward the mastery of material for presentation.

Study carefully the following points in the model outlines:

1. A speech outline should contain five parts: title, introduction, central thought or proposition, development, and conclusion.
2. Standard outlining symbols are used, with subpoints indented to indicate an inferior position:

Fig. 3.6. Covering required material in a limited time is often possible only by closely following the speech outline.

First level: I.
  Second level: A.
   Third level: 1.
    Fourth level: a.
     Fifth level: (1)

3. In the planning stage, complete sentences are used: keep them in declarative form and short.
4. Points are worded in the language which you intend to utter in your speech.
5. Subpoints explain or develop main points.

CHECKING THE SPEECH OUTLINE

You can check the structure of a speech outline by asking yourself the following questions:

1. *Are Points on a Given Level Developed from a Single, Clear Basis of Division?* Earlier in this chapter, several methods of arranging points, or what are called "bases of division," were suggested as possible approaches to the outlining. Mixed classification leads to confusion and fuzzy thinking. In order for points at a given level (I or A or 1, etc.) to be related, coordinate ideas, they should be developed from a single point of view such as physical layout, time order, field of endeavor, parties involved, cause and effect, means and ends, pros and cons. Consider how the following outline violates this requirement:

I. The federal government should control the sale of firearms by mail order, because
   A. Dangerous weapons may fall into the hands of children.
   B. Dangerous weapons are available to subversive groups.
   C. Dangerous weapons contribute to crimes of violence.

Notice that the third reason does not seem to belong with the first two. The first two reasons are from the point of view of the users of firearms; the third from that of results. In other words this outline involves a mixed classification.

2. *Do the Points at a Given Level Overlap?* No two points should cover the same material. The principle is violated if you develop your speech from the point of view of fraternity men, independents, and members of the YMCA; or Republicans, Democrats, and conservatives. The first two in each case are mutually exclusive, but the third is not; for example, a member of the YMCA may be either a fraternity member or an independent.

3. *Are Parallel Points of Equal Value?* A fault of this nature occurs when you make a major point and a subpoint equal in value. Notice the following case.

I. Mile High College should build a larger stadium, because
   A. The present capacity is insufficient to accommodate the students and alumni.
   B. The drinking fountain is inadequate for the visiting teams.
   C. The members of the press cannot see both goal posts.

Point B and probably C are subpoints of a larger, unstated premise which would be on a level of A.

4. *Are Any Subpoints Equal to Main Points?* If a subpoint equals a main point, proper subordination is lacking. Subpoints must support the main point. This fault ordinarily occurs when you merely restate a point and place it under the main point as a reason. The fault is apparent in the following:

I. The Ohio legislature should provide money to build a new student union, because
   A. The old union is inadequate.
   B. A new union should be built.

This second point is not a subpoint, but a restatement of the main proposition.

QUESTIONS FOR INVESTIGATION AND DISCUSSION

1. What is the meaning of the phrase "encodes his message" as used on page 44? If you would like more information on this point, consult David Berlo, *The Process of Communication,* Holt, Rinehart and Winston, 1960, chap. 3, "The Fidelity of Communication."
2. What is oral organization? Is it different from the organization you are encouraged to use in an English composition class? Why would you organize a theme differently from a speech? What type of organization is used in a news story in the daily paper?
3. Are there other schemes of organization not listed on pages 46–49? How and when would you use each of the types listed?
4. What are some schemes for ordering the points of your speech? Are there others besides those mentioned in the chapter?

5. What is psychological organization? How can you organize points according to the inclination of the listeners? See Giles Wilkeson Gray and Waldo W. Braden, *Public Speaking: Principles and Practice* (2nd ed.), Harper & Row, 1963, pp. 249–250.
6. In an informative talk, if you must decide between interest and clarity, which would you choose? How can the two be achieved in the same speech? When is it possible to achieve both?
7. Under what circumstances would you use a one-point speech? In what sense is every effective speech a one-point speech?
8. Why does the central thought of an informative talk differ from the proposition of a persuasive speech?
9. Which of the schemes for determining and arranging points given on pages 46–49 can be applied to a persuasive speech? Which would not be generally useful?
10. What is a *logical* outline? Is the outline for an informative talk a logical outline?
11. How are the three schemes for organizing a persuasive speech related?
12. How are assertive and recommending propositions related?

ASSIGNMENTS

SPEAKING ASSIGNMENTS

1. Deliver a two- to four-minute, how-to-do-it speech. Actually show your classmates how to perform some simple skill or procedure. Attempt to select a subject which will give them information from which they can profit. Do not insult their intelligence by attempting to demonstrate a paper clip, a pencil, a hair curler, etc. Divide your talk into two or three simple steps.

2. Deliver a five-minute informative talk in which you develop three or four points. After a brief introduction, give a preview of your points; as you present each point, write it on the blackboard; in your conclusion, review the points developed by pointing to them as you repeat them orally.

RESEARCH ASSIGNMENT

Work out a new set of examples for the schemes of organization given on pages 44–49.

WRITTEN ASSIGNMENTS

Prepare an outline for an informative speech from the sentences given below. You will, of course, need to put them into some kind of order and to use some statements as subpoints. You need not use every statement; some should be reworded. If you wish to add points you may. Put the outline in the form found on pages 49–50.

Sharpening a Pocket Knife

Do not try to sharpen knives with saw-tooth or serrated edges.
Both sides of a blade should be ground.
Two kinds of sharpeners are useful in sharpening knives: grindstones and oilstones.
Have you ever heard the expression "not sharp enough to cut hot butter"?
Whet on an oilstone in a circular motion, pressing on forward stroke.
You grind on a grindstone and on an oilstone you whet.
It is fun to whittle redwood with a sharpened knife.
Move the blade from side to side when grinding.
Sharpening any kind of knife is not difficult; don't cut yourself.
Tilt edge slowly until grinder reaches the edge.
Take your time.
Lay blade flat and at an angle when whittling.
The best sharpener for a pocket knife is a simple oilstone.
Not all household knives will take edges.
When dull a knife is not very useful.
Hold knife so grindstone will start cutting well back from cutting edge, and then ease toward edge.

2. Prepare an outline for a persuasive talk from the sentences given below (you perhaps have heard many of these statements made with reference to the public schools). Arrange them in a logical order, following the suggestions found on pages 59–60. You may omit any statements you cannot fit into your outline; reword any of them, or add additional points or evidence

Too much time is devoted to football.
The teachers are not stressing the three R's.
The State Superintendent should be appointed, not elected.
The hot lunch program is too expensive.
More funds are needed by the school districts.
Better teachers are needed.
The school boards are politically controlled.
Nothing is too good for our kids.
The bus drivers are underpaid.
No provision is made to help the handicapped.
The teachers haven't had a pay-raise in three years.
An additional one-cent sales tax would produce sufficient revenue to help
  the schools.
The drop-out problem is a disgrace.
Local property taxes are insufficient to support public education.
The state should let the local districts solve their own problems.
Classes of 40 and 50 are too large.
Rumors of cutting the school year to seven months are heard.
Our childen should have the best possible training.
Special classes for the exceptional children are needed.

In class, compare the various outlines which have been prepared. Study carefully how the various students have arranged and subordinated points.

3. Make a detailed outline of a speech published in either *Vital Speeches of the Day* or *Representative American Speeches*.

4. When a speaker divides a central thought or proposition into main points, he should always follow a single principle. In the following examples, determine on what basis the points have been arranged, and check to see whether a single principle has been followed. Correct any faulty analysis.

The students at State College should promote the baseball team.
  The freshmen should promote the team.
  The sophomores should promote the team.
  The fraternities should back the team.

The football squad is composed of the following:
  1. The varsity
  2. The red shirts
  3. The seniors
  4. The freshmen

5. The out-of-state players

You should buy an electric skillet, for
1. It is convenient.
2. It is portable.
3. It is cleaner.
4. You can cook at the table.

You should use a saucepan pressure cooker.
1. It saves time.
2. It saves money.
3. It saves food value.

SUGGESTED READINGS

Borden, Richard C., *Public Speaking—As Listeners Like It!* Harper & Row, 1935.

Braden, Waldo W., and Mary Louise Gehring, *Speech Practices: A Resource Book for the Student of Public Speaking,* Harper & Row, 1958, chap. 3.

Gray, Giles Wilkeson, and Waldo W. Braden, *Public Speaking: Principles and Practice,* Harper & Row, 1963, chap. 14.

Monroe, Alan H., *Principles and Types of Speech* (5th ed.), Scott, Foresman, 1962.

White, Eugene E., *Practical Public Speaking* (2nd ed.), Macmillan, 1964, chap. 5.

Wilson, John F. and Carroll C. Arnold, *Public Speaking As A Liberal Art,* Allyn and Bacon, 1964, chaps. 8 and 9.

❖❖❖ IV

MASTERING YOUR SPEECH

In previous chapters, you have learned how to gather materials and to prepare an outline. By this time you should know what you want to say, and you should have before you a complete outline and the necessary supporting materials. You will remember that you have yet to complete the following:

1. Working on your language
2. Mastering your speech for presentation
3. Perfecting your delivery

Perhaps a good way to see speech preparation as a whole is to study the methods of three prominent speakers.

HOW THREE PROMINENT SPEAKERS
PREPARE THEIR SPEECHES

Richard M. Nixon, Vice President during the Eisenhower Administration, summarizes his preparation which usually takes four or five days in five steps:

1. Doing a great deal of reading in the particular field which I intend to cover.
2. Write down in long hand the various thoughts I think might be worth developing.
3. Make a rough outline in which I try to develop one central theme.
4. Make usually three or four more outlines, the final one is almost a complete copy of the speech.
5. Dictate a draft into the dictaphone . . . ; some changes may occur.[1]

Now let us review how Bishop Fulton J. Sheen, famous radio and television preacher, prepares for his appearances on the air.

His telecasts are usually broadcast on Tuesday evenings in New York. On the following morning he starts preparing for his next talk by devoting his Wednesday holy hour to meditation on three or four possible and promising topics. . . . He rejects more ideas than he uses. Later on in the day a skeleton outline of the topic is written and immediately destroyed.

For several days he will let his mind lie fallow (fallow, that is, according to his standards). But on Monday, the day before the telecast, he is ready to consider the subject. He begins with one of his "rehearsals." Walking up and down in his study, he speaks a program out loud for half an hour. At least thirty hours are spent preparing each program. He writes and tears up a dozen outlines. He gives his talk once in French to a Frenchman, and once in Italian to an Italian. The night before the program he delivers it in English to a group of nuns.[2]

---

[1] Quoted in Ben Padrow and Bruce Richards, "Richard Nixon. . . . His Speech Preparation," *Today's Speech*, **VII** (November, 1959), 11–12.

[2] Nelson Hart, "Bishop Sheen's Television Techniques," *Today's Speech*, **X** (September, 1962), 18–19.

Fig. 4.1. Richard Nixon, Bishop Sheen, and Senator Morse each prepares his speech in his own unique way, yet each includes oral practice as an important ingredient in mastery.

Equally interesting is the method of Senator Wayne Morse, fiery independent Democrat from Oregon:

> The steps that I go through in preparing a formal address are very simple. (1) I study the subject. (2) I collect the data and material that I'm going to use in the speech content. (3) I prepare an outline of the speech, or if it is to be a written speech, I usually dictate it to a secretary. . . . As my secretaries would tell you, what I really do is make the speech to them and they take it down. Very seldom does any sentence of my dictated speeches have to be changed.
>
> I suppose my habits in connection with preparing speeches go back to an interesting study habit that I developed from the time I was in grade school. I used to ride long distances to school on horseback, eleven miles each way. And I developed the habit of preparing many of my lessons, recitations, and—later—speeches riding along on horseback—and frequently thinking out loud. Even to this day I frequently on weekends will take a long horseback ride and prepare my speech in the saddle based upon reading that I've already done on the subject. The next day I find that I am able to give that speech on the floor of the Senate with what I'm sure would be hardly a word changed if it could be compared with the speech that I wrote in my mind the day before on a three or four hour horseback ride. Or I can sit at home the night before and work out a speech in my mind and then walk into the office the next morning and dictate it off to my secretary almost as though I were reading it from a handwritten manuscript. . . .[3]

After reading these statements, it is evident that each man prepares a speech in his own unique way. However, they all utilize several of the steps which have already been discussed. You can learn much from the three. It is doubtful whether many can give their speeches to dictaphones, or rehearse in three languages as is Sheen's custom, or whether many will have the opportunity to prepare on horseback. But you can certainly rehearse orally, which seems to be a common practice with all three.

[3] Wayne Morse, quoted in Emery V. Hildebrandt, "Senator Wayne Morse on Speech Preparation," *Today's Speech*, VI (April, 1958), 8.

MASTERY OF SHORT SPEECHES

To Write or Not to Write

The novice is likely to inquire whether he can save time by first writing out his remarks in full. For *most short speeches,* you will probably find this step unnecessary and, in some cases, even a handicap. You may spend hours in polishing your language, and then find that when you face your listeners you become hesitant and indirect in your struggle to recall the exact words over which you have spent so much loving care. More important, you need to develop the ability to think on your feet, because circumstances may not always permit you the time for elaborate preparation. You should develop the habit of extemporizing. Wisely planned oral rehearsals will give you mastery over your materials.

It is true that some persons find that writing helps to crystallize ideas, to plan the sequence of presentation, and to refine language. They remember with Bacon that "writing maketh an exact man." This practice becomes increasingly important for longer speeches.

Should You Memorize Your Speeches?

This is the next logical question. For most speakers the answer is an emphatic *no.* Complete and word-perfect memorization is tedious and difficult for many persons. It often adds the fear of forgetting and thus to stage fright. The process of "thinking on your feet" creates a highly desirable directness and makes communication easier.

How Should You Use a Manuscript?

If you write a manuscript, as a step in the mastery of ideas, you should read it aloud several times, then lay it aside, and force yourself to think through the development of your ideas. This step takes real fortitude; it will take even more not to succumb to the temptation of returning to the manuscript. If you carry it to the platform, you are sure to want to peek at it occasionally, and you may even end up reading it. The result is likely to be indirectness and lack of communicativeness.

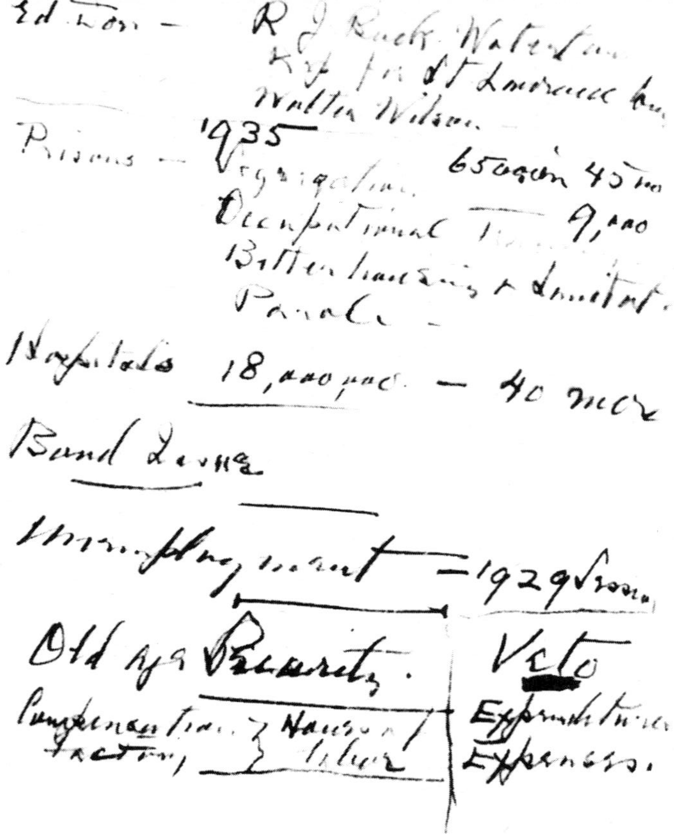
Testimonial Dinner

TO

Franklin D. Roosevelt

GOVERNOR OF THE STATE OF NEW YORK

By

Democratic Club *of* Oneida County, Inc.

MONDAY, JUNE THE NINTH,
Nineteen Hundred and Thirty

HOTEL UTICA
Utica, New York

Fig. 4.2 Franklin D. Roosevelt's speaker notes. (*Franklin D. Roosevelt Library, Hyde Park, New York*)

Take a tip from Sheen and Morse: Work through *oral rehearsal;* practice it on your feet, simulating actual delivery to a live audience. Prepare some speaker's notes which include a suggestion of your main points and any detailed material which may give you difficulty in remembering. These notes are to give you confidence, to relieve you of the fear of forgetting. You will need to do some experimentation to discover what kind works best for you,[4] but the following is one example:

SPEAKER'S NOTES

Seat Belt

5000 lives saved each year.
Seat belts save lives.

    I. Prevent being ejected
       60% safer
       Risk 5 times greater when ejected
   II. Reduces impact
  III. Prevents being wrenched from wheel
AMA and NSC agree about belts

You may wish to memorize the exact wordings of your main points in order to set the structure of your presentation (for form, see pages 54–55).

You will probably find three or four oral rehearsals at spaced intervals excellent for adequate preparation. Five, half-hour workouts are probably superior to two and a half hours of continuous practice. Actors discover that "walking through" their scenes, associating their words with stage business and movement and with the lines of other actors, makes memorizing easier. Actually, the same is true in preparing a speech. You should rehearse the presentation of charts, blackboard drawings, and models as a part of your preparation.

[4] For samples of speaker's notes used by prominent speakers, see Waldo W. Braden and Mary Louise Gehring, *Speech Practices: A Resource Book for the Student of Public Speaking,* Harper & Row, 1958, pp. 35–48.

A PLAN FOR ORAL REHEARSAL

The First Rehearsal

This first practice period will involve the fumbling stage. Completion of your speech may take two or three times as long as you will have for the final delivery. Don't be afraid to talk around the subject. Keep asking yourself, "How will my listeners react to what I am saying?" Experiment with different approaches in presenting points. Work on emphasis, control of bodily action, and manipulation of visual aids. You undoubtedly will have many vocalized pauses and broken rhythm. As you grope to find the right word, follow your outline and concentrate on your thought.

The Second Rehearsal

This practice should ideally take place several hours after the first session. You will discover now that your language comes a little easier, and that you have fewer vocalized pauses. Continue your experimentation, but now you should begin to think seriously about your time limit. Concentrate on what is essential to put over your message.

The Third Rehearsal

In many cases, the third practice session will be the final one. During this period, attempt to present your talk the way you intend to do it before the listeners. By this time, you should be able to manipulate all the visual aids and equipment with ease and assurance. To this final practice, you may want to invite a colleague or friend to listen to you. Sympathetic listeners can help you to work on directness. You may even record the speech. *Your goal is not to memorize* your remarks; you will discover, however, that by this time you have developed certain key phrases, and some sentences will come to you without an effort on your part to remember. It is extremely important that you continue to concentrate on your thought development.

Fig. 4.3. Oral rehearsal can utilize any handy auditor! Do not memorize but let your ideas and their sequence reinforce themselves in your mind as you practice.

If you are not confident, if you run too far over the time limit, or if you are dissatisfied with your plan and decide upon a new approach, you will need additional oral rehearsals.

In the process of creating a speech you should avoid *constant* evaluation of your progress, for in many cases it fosters dissatisfac-

tion and discouragement. In support of this suggestion, Knight
Dunlap says:

> Ideals, purposes, and plans are the indispensable conditions of effective
> learning. These, however, do their work best when let alone. Constant
> purposing, constant planning, constant determining of ideals are dam-
> aging. These important operations should be undertaken at specific times,
> with reference to definite succeeding periods, and then dropped from
> thought.[5]

A Final Rundown

Shortly before you speak, you will perhaps find it helpful to
review your complete outline. Check yourself on the following
questions:

1. Do I know my goal?
2. Do I have my strategy clearly in mind?
3. Can I repeat my main points or are my speaker's notes clear?
4. Can I see my speech as a whole?

An Important Don't

Just before the delivery of the speech, don't push the panic button.
In other words, do not attempt a hurried, frustrated, last-minute
rehearsal in desperation. If you feel uneasy, try harder to create an
eagerness to speak. As you wait for your turn, give attention to:

1. What have previous speakers said?
2. Is there anything in their talks that refers to yours?
3. Is there a pleasant way to bridge the gap between what they
   are saying and what you intend to say?
4. How has your introducer helped or made it more difficult for you?
5. Are there any specific problems in the speaking environment
   with which you must cope?

[5] Knight Dunlap, *Habits: Their Making and Unmaking*, Liveright, 1932, p.
162.

THE ROLE OF MEMORY

Quintilian declared memory to be "the treasury of eloquence," while Cicero referred to it as "the treasury and guardian of all things." Indeed, your speaking effectiveness often depends upon whether you can marshal accurately and quickly your materials at the moment of utterance. "I didn't say half of what I wanted to," or "I forgot my most important point," or "My speech was nothing like what I had intended," are signs of a memory problem.

Memory is the capacity to remember or to use what has been learned. Actually, within this process are three closely associated phases:

1. Memorizing or learning the material
2. Retention for a period of time
3. Remembering or reproducing when needed

These three aspects—memorizing, retention, and remembering—are important in a speech. Quintilian said that memory "brings before us those multitudes of precedents, laws, judgments, sayings, and facts, of which an orator should have an abundance, and which he should always be ready to produce."[6] In addition to reproducing facts, memory involves the recall of previously prepared materials, namely, the plan of development, the order of the points, the specific supports, inclusion of visual aids, the language, and the planned mode of physical and vocal behavior.

Different degrees of preparation place varying demands upon the mastery process. The carefully prepared speech, naturally, contains more elements for recall than the one thrown together hastily. In an extempore effort you must remember your previously prepared plan, forms of support, planned mode of behavior. In addition to these elements, the memorized speech demands recall of the verbatim wording. Let us, therefore, consider in more detail the preparation of the impromptu, the extemporaneous, the manuscript, and the memorized speech.

[6] Quintilian, *Institutes of Oratory*, (Trans. John Selby Watson), Bohn, 1856, Vol. II, 333.

The Impromptu Speech

You may think that mastery is not a factor in the unprepared, spur-of-the-moment speech in which you must collect, organize, and present your thoughts almost simultaneously. It is true that you have no previous opportunity to memorize, but you do exercise recall when you pull together your materials.

At such a time you will find great comfort in a large storehouse of information and a broad background of reading and experience. But background is not enough. If you are to summon up your thoughts and materials, you must first free yourself of the consternation that strikes when you are singled out to speak. If you are so busy thinking about yourself, you cannot concentrate upon your subject; consequently, you experience what the psychologist refers to as emotional interference. Woodworth explains, "Fear may paralyze recall. Anxious self-consciousness or stage fright has prevented the recall of many a well-learned speech, and disturbed many a well-practiced act."[7]

A second type of interference occurs at the instant you have difficulty deciding what thoughts to present, particularly if two or more ways of expressing an idea come into your mind at the same time. As a consequence, you are faced with indecision, become hesitant, and utter meaningless "and-a's" and "uh's" and incoherent thoughts.

How can you relieve yourself of these tensions? The best general preparation for impromptu speaking is frequent practice in extempore speaking. In this manner, you develop confidence in your ability to phrase your ideas meaningfully under pressure, in spite of your fears. You discover and practice ways to tie your thoughts into what has been said by previous speakers, and into what has happened at the moment.

The following additional suggestions may further help you to overcome fears and to concentrate upon what to say.

1. When you are called upon to speak, immediately start searching in what has already been said for an opening remark. Do you

[7] Robert S. Woodworth, *Psychology* (4th ed.), Holt, Rinehart and Winston, 1940, p. 350.

agree or disagree with the previous speakers? Has the chairman said something that you can use? Why have you been called upon to speak? What has the previous speaker said that you can further develop?

2. In order to avoid indecision about what to say, attempt immediately to formulate a concise answer to the stated problem. Put your answer into a single short sentence, and then develop it. You may start your impromptu remarks in the following manner: "You have asked me how to increase production on the night shift. It is my opinion that we need a complete reorganization of our personnel." Notice that the first sentence relates the speech to what the chairman has asked and that the second is a concise statement of what you intend to discuss. On another occasion, you might open by saying, "For the last thirty minutes we have been discussing the advisability of constructing a new school building. From what has been said it is evident to me that we must have a new school. The only problem now is how much shall we invest in this project."

The formula for opening an impromptu speech may be summarized as follows:

a. Relate speech to what has been said
    (1) by a previous speaker
    (2) by an authority
    (3) by the chairman
b. State concisely your point of view.
c. Give some illustrations and examples to support your answer.

3. What we have advised on stage fright in Chapter I is equally applicable here. By concentrating upon your subject and not permitting yourself to think about yourself, you have a better opportunity to speak more intelligently on your subject.

4. Attempt to create a favorable impression in opening your remarks. Don't advertise your nervousness with an opening apology: "I just don't know what I can say on the subject," "I am sure someone else knows more about this question than I do," or "I don't feel qualified to discuss the topic, but . . ." Likewise, in concluding, avoid apologetic statements such as the following: "Now let me see if there is anything else that I should say," "That is about all I can think of," or "I hope that is what you wanted from me."

Fig. 4.4. Vice President Hubert Humphrey is recognized as a witty and resourceful extemporaneous speaker.

The Extemporaneous Speech

Quintilian observed that "the ability of speaking extempore" depends on "no other faculty of mind" than memory.[8] The extemporaneous speech should embrace careful planning and thorough rehearsal, but it does not require an attempt to set the language prior to your speech. Therefore, at the moment of presentation, you must recall only your organization, supporting materials, and planned mode of delivery.

It becomes apparent that much of what has been said in earlier chapters might be repeated in this section. For the sake of review, let us summarize some of these mastery aids:

1. Memorize the main points expressed in the form you intend to use in your speech. These key sentences more firmly establish a chain of association which binds the speech together and hence aids recall.
2. The parallel wording of main points, the use of signposts, and the employment of other transitional devices also strengthen the chain of association. In the same sense, the preview and pattern

[8] Quintilian, *loc. cit.*

Fig. 4.5. A manuscript requires hours of research, rewriting, and rereading.

    of development serve as much as memory aids as they do for clarity.

3. The oral preparation, in which you rehearse your speech aloud simulating delivery before an audience, is based upon equally sound learning principles.

4. The more you talk about a subject in conversation, in round-table discussions, before clubs, or in the classroom, the less trouble you will have with recall.

5. Oral rehearsal of a speech at regularly spaced intervals makes learning easier and further assures retention.

The Manuscript Speech

    Many persons in positions of leadership or high trust often find themselves called upon to speak about subjects of considerable consequence. What is to be said will be interpreted as a statement of policy. For example, the President of the United States often must choose his words thoughtfully, for what he says will be analyzed around the word as a pronouncement of the government of the United States. He and his advisers take many hours to prepare his statements. A slip of the tongue may affect foreign relations in a dozen capitals overseas. These and similar occasions demand manuscripts. Radio and television also demand a manuscript because broadcasters cannot risk putting on the air material that has not been carefully checked and timed.

Is mastery a problem in this situation? In truth, memory problems are greatly reduced, for you do not have to recall materials which are immediately before you. If you wish, you may read them word for word without lifting your eyes from your prepared copy or from the teleprompter; but as a result, you sacrifice directness, and you will have difficulty developing rapport. On the other hand, if you look at your listeners occasionally, you must be able to look away from your manuscript while speaking. Herein is a real problem. You must increase your powers of recognition and develop within the manuscript as many reading cues as possible.

Below are some suggestions which should help you in preparing your manuscript for effective delivery:

1. Type your manuscript with double or triple spaces, without too many words to the line and with ample margins on all sides. Do not divide words at the ends of sentences, and do not divide sentences at the bottoms of pages. Use short paragraphs.
2. Strive to write the way you speak.
3. Underline, or type in red, signposts for key parts of the speech. This will enable you to note your progress and to return to your place in case you wish to extemporize from your manuscript.
4. Read and reread your speech until you are thoroughly familiar with it, partially memorizing many passages.
5. Actually plan where in the manuscript you intend to look up from your reading copy; then practice looking at your simulated listeners.
6. You may wish to memorize completely occasional passages so that during delivery you can give the impression of extemporizing upon your subject.

The Memorized Passage or Speech

At times you may find advantage in memorizing an introduction, a speech of presentation, a speech of welcome or farewell, or some other type of short speech. Or you may wish to memorize an important passage, an introduction, conclusion, or an apt quotation. In these particular situations, you will put your memory to a severe test because you must have perfect recall.

When should you attempt to memorize? To put the answer briefly, when you are alert, at ease, and rested. If you are tired or harassed about other matters, you will have difficulty concentrating and you will tend to wander away from the passage under consideration. In order to conserve energy, therefore, carefully select your study periods.

For short units, the *whole* method of memorizing is generally considered superior to the *part* method; that is, you commit to memory a whole passage instead of attempting to master lines or sentences and then assembling them into a whole. Through the whole method, you can establish a strong train of association and make transitions with greater ease and with less risk of forgetting.

In using the whole method, follow these steps:

1. First read the entire selection for understanding, noting how the passage is put together, the pattern of partition, and how the points are arranged.
2. In memorizing the writing of another person, you may discover real advantage in attempting to place the selection in its proper context, acquainting yourself with the author, with the sources of his ideas, and with chapter or section from which a specific line or sentence is lifted.
3. When you understand the material, put the manuscript or book aside and attempt to reconstruct the selection as a whole, perhaps even summarize it orally.
4. Reread the manuscript several times, simulating how you intend to deliver it and, of course, using a conversational approach. Stay on your feet while working, and associate gestures and bodily movement with the various thoughts and points of emphasis.
5. Practice for several short periods in preference to fewer longer periods.
6. Lay aside the manuscript as soon as possible and force yourself to recall, no matter how hesitant you may seem.
7. To ensure accuracy, have someone check your delivery against

This theme has been that Americans are admittedly rich, and that Americans have considerable industrial power -- but that Americans are soft and decadent, that they cannot and will not united and work and fight.

From Berlin, Rome and Tokyo we have been described as a nation of weaklings -- "playboys" -- who would hire British soldiers, or Russian soldiers, or Chinese soldiers to do our fighting for us.

Let them repeat that now!

Let them tell that to General MacArthur and his men.

Let them tell that to the sailors who today are hitting hard in the far waters of the Pacific.

Let them tell that to the boys in the Flying Fortresses.

Let them tell that to the Marines!

Franklin Roosevelt Library, Hyde Park, New York

Fig. 4.6. A portion of the reading copy of a speech F.D.R. delivered on February 23, 1942. Notice how the lines are spaced.

And General Washington ordered that these great words written by Tom Paine be read to the men of every regiment in the Continental Army, and this was the assurance given to the first American armed forces:

"The summer soldier and the sunshine patriot will, in this crisis, shrink from the service of their country; but he that stands it now, deserves the love and thanks of man and woman. Tyranny, like hell, is not easily conquered; yet we have this consolation with us, that the harder the sacrifice, the more glorious the triumph".

So spoke Americans in the year 1776.

So speak Americans today!

****

Franklin D. Roosevelt

Big reading copy

Fig. 4.6. (*Continued*)

the manuscript or book. Make yourself strain, however, to remember, and do not permit prompting until you are sure you can reproduce the thought.

The best insurance against forgetting is overlearning, or "learning beyond the point when it can barely be reproduced."[9] Overlearning of speech materials is particularly important for effective delivery. If you are to give the impression that you are spontaneously conversing with your listeners, you must not have to struggle to recall words, phrases, and sentences. When the memorizing is imperfectly done, you ordinarily lose your urge to communicate, with the result that you concentrate upon recall instead of upon "putting over" your thoughts.

One of the most difficult problems in delivering memorized or partially memorized material is to maintain what is commonly referred to as "the illusion of the first time," giving the impression of spontaneous and thoughtful presentation. As Charles H. Woolbert observed:

. . . The great majority of speeches which are committed word for word are remote from the audience, strained, unnatural, even affected. It takes an artist to deliver a memorized speech well; the tendency always is to quit thinking while thus reciting and so to break up the fine adjustment between thinking, voice, and body necessary for vital speaking.[10]

If naturalness and directness are to be achieved, you must set your vocal and bodily patterns as well as your thoughts and words. Memorizing aloud and attempting during practice to simulate a speaking situation is most important. Memory failures result in such problems as:

1. Speaking too rapidly
2. Emphasizing words of little importance
3. Repeating words and phrases
4. Falling into monotonous vocal patterns
5. Speaking with little facial expression

[9] Woodworth, op. cit., p. 348.
[10] Charles Henry Woolbert, The Fundamentals of Speech (rev. ed.), Harper & Row, 1927, p. 372.

6. Failing to synchronize gestures with the presentation of thoughts
7. Neglecting to adjust the loudness of the voice to the room

Breaking Memory Blocks

In the midst of a speech, a speaker sometimes "goes blank," meaning that he experiences memory failure. What can you do to break a memory block? Frequently this question is posed by students who participate in speech contests, by persons who have difficulty recalling names, by those who are absent-minded, and by many others. As already pointed out, "overlearning" is the best insurance against forgetting, but in spite of such efforts, you may suffer occasional lapses of memory.

Seemingly, no magic formula exists to ensure you against such difficulties. As a rule, however, if you permit memory failure to stir you up emotionally, you intensify the problems of recovery when you have a memory lapse, you will be wise not to attempt to force yourself to remember. Shift your attention momentarily away from the matter; in a moment you may recall the desired item. Many persons have difficulty remembering names and faces. Try as you will, the name won't come, but five minutes later, when you have turned to other things, you know the name. Speakers who forget often find that it helps to walk around a moment and then start again on a paragraph preceding the place where the forgetting occurred. If you think about the thoughts as they occur without trying to think ahead to the troublesome spot, by the time you arrive again at the difficult place, you can bridge the gap without difficulty.

QUESTIONS FOR INVESTIGATION AND DISCUSSION

1. What points in common do Nixon, Sheen, and Morse follow in their speech preparation?
2. What steps does each take in mastering his speeches for presentation?
3. What are their individual differences in speech preparation?

4. What are the advantages and disadvantages of writing out your speech in its entirety? (See what other textbooks say.)
5. What types of speeches might it be advisable to memorize?
6. Why should the speaker use some type of oral rehearsal? From the point of view of learning, what are the advantages?
7. What steps would you pursue in preparing for a second presentation of the same speech?
8. If you were delivering the same speech a second time, would additional oral rehearsal be necessary?
9. What is memory? Investigate several sources before you attempt to answer.
10. How is memory important in the public-speaking process?
11. How has the role of memory in speechmaking changed through the ages? What modern devices have been developed to solve the problems of memory?
12. What are some typical memory problems that a speaker faces?
13. Is the use of the word *memory* in this chapter the same as current usage?
14. Why have textbooks on public speaking generally omitted considerations of memory?
15. What are some of the methods for improving memory recommended by popular memory courses? Are any of these suggestions applicable to public speaking?
16. Under what conditions is memory likely to fail the public speaker?
17. How can a speaker give himself memory aids in preparing his manuscript?
18. In what sense can broad knowledge improve the memory potential of a public speaker?

ASSIGNMENTS

SPEAKING ASSIGNMENTS

1. Deliver a 10-minute report on one of the following topics or a similar one:

a. How a famous speech was prepared
b. How a prominent speaker prepares his speeches
c. How poor speech preparation caused a speaker to fail
d. A sure-fire method of speech preparation
e. Famous speech ghost writers
f. Ghost writing today
g. Speech writing teams of recent Presidents

2. Your instructor will draw up a list of speaking topics from recent issues of a local newspaper or news magazine. He will prepare as many topic slips as there are students in the class and place them face down on a table. When your turn to speak comes, you are to go to the table, pick up three topics, select one, and replace the other two. You then are to discuss the topic you have drawn.

RESEARCH ASSIGNMENTS

1. Interview a local minister or some prominent local speaker concerning his methods of speech preparation. (Your instructor will tell you whether the results of the interview are to be submitted orally to the class or in written report.) Ask the interviewee such questions as:

a. How does the speaker get ideas for speeches?
b. Does he keep a speech materials file or scrap book?
c. What sources has he found the best for supplying ideas and materials for speeches?
d. What steps does he follow in preparing a speech?
e. In his preparation, does he prepare an outline, write a complete manuscript, memorize it?
f. Does he rehearse it orally? Does he have anyone who acts as a critic? Does he use a speech recorder in speech preparation?
g. Does he have any advice about speech preparation which he would give to beginning speakers?

2. Investigate how a famous speaker prepared his speeches, considering questions given in the first research assignment.
3. Locate and report some popular memory schemes. You may have one of your own, or your friends or teachers may have

developed methods. Also investigate the method taught in popular personality courses.

BULLETIN BOARD ASSIGNMENT

Theme: Famous Orators of the Past (search through *Life* Magazine).

SUGGESTED READINGS

Braden, Waldo W., "The Bases of William E. Borah's Speech Preparation," *Quarterly Journal of Speech,* **XXXIII** (February, 1947), 28–30.

Braden, Waldo W., and Mary Louise Gehring, *Speech Practices: A Resource Book for the Student of Public Speaking,* Harper & Row, 1958, chaps. 2 and 3.

Brandenburg, Earnest, "The Preparation of Franklin D. Roosevelt's Speeches," *Quarterly Journal of Speech,* **XXXV** (April, 1949), 214–221.

Crowell, Laura, "Building the 'Four Freedoms' Speech," *Speech Monographs,* **XXII** (November, 1955), 266–283.

Feris, Frances, "The Speech Preparation of John Bright," *Quarterly Journal of Speech,* **XVII** (November, 1931), 492–504.

Hart, Nelson, "Bishop Sheen's Television Techniques," *Today's Speech,* **X** (September, 1962), 18–21.

Hildebrandt, Emery V., "Senator Wayne Morse on Speech Preparation," *Today's Speech,* **VI** (April, 1958), 7–9.

Hopkins, Thomas A., "Attorney-General Robert F. Kennedy's Blueprint for Civil Rights Action," *Today's Speech,* **X** (February, 1962), 5–7.

Lomas, Charles W., and Ralph Richardson, *Speech: Idea and Delivery* (2nd ed.), Houghton Mifflin, 1963.

McGlon, Charles A., "How I Prepare My Sermons: A Symposium," *Quarterly Journal of Speech,* **XL** (February, 1954), pp. 49–62.

Padrow, Ben, and Adrian Emery, "George Romney: From the Mission to the Mansion," *Today's Speech,* **XII** (February, 1964), 2–3.

Padrow, Ben, and Bruce Richards, "Richard Nixon—His Speech Preparation," *Today's Speech*, **VII** (November, 1959), 11–12.

Reid, Loren D., "Did Charles Fox Prepare His Speeches?" *Quarterly Journal of Speech*, **XXIV** (February, 1938), 17–26.

Reid, Loren D., "Gladstone's Essay on Public Speaking," *Quarterly Journal of Speech*, **XXXIX** (October, 1953), 265–272.

Tacey, William S., "Clarence B. Randall: Spokesman for Industry," *Today's Speech*, **VI** (November, 1958), 6–8.

White, Eugene E., and Clair R. Henderlider, "What Harry S. Truman Told Us About His Speaking," *Quarterly Journal of Speech*, **XL** (February, 1954), 37–42.

White, Eugene E., and Clair R. Henderlider, "What Norman Vincent Peale Told Us About His Speaking," *Quarterly Journal of Speech*, **XL** (December, 1954), 407–416.

READINGS ON MEMORY

Crocker, Lionel, *Public Speaking for College Students* (3rd ed.), American Book Company, 1956, chap. 8.

Dunlap, Knight, *Habits—Their Making and Unmaking*, Liveright, 1932, chaps. 7 and 8.

Hoffman, William G., *Public Speaking for Business Men* (3rd ed.), McGraw-Hill, 1949, chap. 6.

Hoogestraat, Wayne E., "Memory: The Lost Canon?" *Quarterly Journal of Speech*, **XLVI** (April, 1960), 141–147.

Scott, Walter Dill, *The Psychology of Public Speaking*, Pearson Brothers, 1907, chaps. 13, 14.

Smith, Bromley, "Hippias and a Lost Canon of Rhetoric," *Quarterly Journal of Speech*, **XII** (June, 1926), 129–145.

Wells, Earl W., "Methods of Memorization For the Speaker and Reader," *Quarterly Journal of Speech*, **XIV** (February, 1928), 39–64.

V

SELLING YOURSELF
TO YOUR LISTENERS

In the fourth century B.C., Aristotle wrote one of the world's great books on public speaking. Much of what he said is as fresh and applicable today as it was in those ancient times. After considerable observation and thought, that learned Greek concluded that *moral* character (ethos) constitutes the most effective or potent means of persuasion; Aristotle place it even above emotional and logical appeals. He explained that the speaker persuades by moral character "when he speaks in a manner as to render him worthy of confidence."[1]

[1] Aristotle, *"Art" of Rhetoric* (Trans. John Henry Freese), Harvard Univ. Press, 1926, p. 17.

Abraham Lincoln recommended that "to convince a man that you are his sincere friend . . . is the great high road to reason," provided your cause is really a just one.[2] This tremendous principle, known for so long, has had little influence on some contemporary speakers, who still put their faith in tricks and gimmicks instead of in solid character.

Thus, to gain the confidence of your listeners—a necessary first step in speaking—involves your reputation, your appearance, and ethical appeal.

REPUTATION

Now let us turn our attention to a consideration of the first element of gaining a friendly hearing. To win your way, you must start with a clear view of how your listeners regard you as a person and as a speaker. In other words you need to ascertain what your reputation is with your listeners. When the President of the United States speaks, he is usually assured of million of listeners here and abroad. Why? He need not be a great speaker to win a hearing, as several presidents have proved. The mere prestige of his office and importance of his decisions pulls millions to their radios and television sets to hear him. Under these conditions a long speech of introduction is unnecessary. Thus, at its most superficial level, reputation is a most influential factor in his appeal.

In recent presidential elections, for example, the reputation of candidates markedly influenced campaign techniques and probably the election outcomes as well. In 1952, Dwight Eisenhower brought into the campaign unusual appeal. As an already revered figure, he attracted voters; consequently, he overshadowed the more eloquent Adlai Stevenson. In 1956, Vice President Richard Nixon was suspect because he had the reputation of being considered a master of invective, an effective phrase maker, and name caller.[3] During the campaign he realized the need to change this image, and he sought

---

[2] Abraham Lincoln, "Temperance Address," *The Collected Works of Abraham Lincoln*, Roy P. Basler (Ed.), Rutgers Univ. Press, 1953, I, 271–279.

[3] See William Lee Miller, "The Debating Career of Richard M. Nixon," *The Reporter*, April 19, 1956, pp. 11–17.

Fig. 5.1. "Kennedy gained votes by his youthful face, his trim look, and his ready smile." (H. L. Harding)

Wide World

to present himself as a sincere, dignified, and forthright public servant. He knew that reputation—or what Aristotle called "antecedent impression"—was an important factor in winning public support.

Here are some important questions to ask yourself about your reputation before you speak:

1. How familiar are my listeners with my background and qualifications?
2. What are their sources of information? Friends? Opponents? Hearsay?
3. Are my listeners favorably or unfavorably disposed toward me as a speaker? Why? How can I use their attitudes in my speech?
4. What aspects of my background do I (or my introducer) need to emphasize?
5. Do I need to establish that I am qualified to speak on the subject? that I am a man of good character? that I am of good will toward my listeners?

YOUR APPEARANCE

An important part of selling yourself to any audience has to do with your appearance. You communicate not only through language, but also through what you wear and what you do. Your listeners may decide before you utter a word whether they like you and whether they intend to hear you out. As they listen to what you say, they continue to study your general appearance, your clothes, your platform manner. They will note careless or inappropriate dress; for example, to appear in tuxedo before a rural group or in overalls before a downtown Kiwanis Club is likely to cost you a favorable hearing. Patently false eyelashes or bleached hair may have an immediate adverse effect on your reception in many women's groups. In 1960, there was much talk about John Kennedy's youthfulness, and the Republicans quickly seized the opportunity to insist that the country needed mature, experienced leadership. The turn of events is interesting. One columnist observed that "Mr. Kennedy conveyed an impression of *intensity* and *grasp of his subject* which tends to overcome his relative *youthfulness*."[4] Kennedy also changed his haircut to a more mature style.

Another observer summarized Kennedy's problems with appearance as follows:

Kennedy . . . started the campaign as the less well-known candidate and with many of his adherents wondering about his maturity. He has done a good job dissipating the immaturity label and has increased his standing on every issue test. Kennedy has succeeded in creating a victory psychology.[5]

Appearance caused Nixon difficulty, too. In his first debate with Kennedy, the Vice President appeared "haggard and worn," "tired, drawn and . . . ill." His difficulty resulted from his black beard, poor makeup, inadequate lighting, and weariness from illness and overwork. Quite naturally, Republicans became extremely concerned

[4] Roscoe Drummond, *Christian Science Monitor*, September 24, 1960.
[5] Earl Mazo, *The Great Debates, An Occasional Paper on the Role of the Political Process in Free Society*, Center for Study of Democratic Institutions, 1962, p. 4.

because of the contrast with the youthful, energetic Kennedy. They were fearful that the listeners were more conscious of Nixon's appearance than "of what he was saying."[6]

Your image is important! A good rule is to strive to conform to what your listeners consider acceptable appearance and manner. "In Rome, do as the Romans do."

Before speaking, you should thoughtfully review the following questions:

1. How do my listeners regard me? Youthful? Middle aged? Old?
2. What is my public image with my listeners? Favorable? Neutral? Unfavorable?
3. What limitations does the speaking environment place upon me as to wearing apparel and manner?
4. What is considered appropriate or acceptable dress and deportment?
5. Are there any impressions about me for which I need to compensate?

ESTABLISHING YOUR RIGHT TO SPEAK

Aristotle says that there are three sources of a speaker's credibility: good sense, good moral character, and good will. These three aspects are "the great high road" to acceptance and influence.[7]

To whom do you go for advice? If your problem is important, you select a friend who is well informed, who perhaps has special insights, and who can apply his knowledge to the solution of your problem. Now turn this analysis around. Your listeners are going to look for those same qualities in you as a speaker. If you appear to be well informed, a man of good sense and practical wisdom, you will have no problems in winning a friendly and attentive hearing.

If your listeners do not know why you are peculiarly well fitted to discuss your subject, then you must somehow take care of the void, giving assurance that you are worth listening to and that you have

[6] Herbert A. Seltz and Richard D. Yoakam, "Production Diary of the Debates" in Sidney Kraus (Ed.), *The Great Debate,* Indiana University Press, 1962, p. 95.

[7] Aristotle, *op. cit.,* p. 171.

earned the right to speak on your subject. You may stress your sagacity or good sense indirectly through what you put into your speech, or you (or the person who introduces you) may make direct reference to your experience.

Your listeners may evaluate your intelligence on the following bases:

1. Whether you are forthright in giving the sources of your materials
2. Whether your ideas and supporting materials are specific, coherent, and internally consistent
3. Whether your interpretations and supporting materials are original and pertinent
4. Whether your command of language and pronunciation are consistent with that of an educated man
5. Whether your voice seems "cultured and refined"
6. Whether your development suggests extensive reflection and careful preparation

Of course your listeners will also judge you by the degree of confidence in yourself that you demonstrate, and in the ways you label what you say. Such expressions as "in my opinion," "according to theory," "someone told me," "my research shows" reflect upon your insights and the ways you arrived at your conclusions.

However, to establish that you have earned the right to speak, you or your introducer may want to make direct reference to your qualifications and experience. A simple statement about background and preparation will not be regarded as immodest or improper; quite the contrary, it may assist the listener to evaluate what you are about to say. Below are several sentences which illustrate how direct references have been made to a person's qualifications:

I have just left your fighting sons in Korea . . . (*Douglas MacArthur*).

As State Senator, as Governor, and as a member of the U.S. Senate, I have been interested . . . for more than 40 years . . . (*Senator Harry Byrd*).

What I saw and heard as I traveled this vast territory that lies under the southern rim of Russia . . . (*Associate Justice William O. Douglas*).

Fig. 5.2. Margaret Chase Smith's extensive and varied experiences helped to establish her right to speak.

During the past six months, I made two overseas trips . . . to twenty-three countries covering fifty thousand miles (*Senator Margaret Chase Smith*).

Some additional examples are:

The computer at General Electric has just determined that. . . .
I have lived and worked with the Russians.
Through years of investigations, I have learned many new things.
Our findings are based on the latest research.
Several authorities have confirmed my conclusions.
After a year-long study, we determined that. . . .

Notice how these three speakers establish their right to speak upon their subjects:

I have just completed an informal review of Alliance for Progress problems with all the ambassadors and the distinguished head of C.I.A.P.,

Carlo Sanz de Santamaria. This kind of exchange strengthens our common aim and our combined ability to advance the Alliance.[8]

It may seem presumptuous for me to discuss the nation and philosophy of law, because my slender means as a youth did not permit me to study it formally. But, in modest qualification, I have had over fifty years of experience in and around lawmakers, who are sometimes—and with understandable irreverence—called politicians. I am a politician—and I am proud of it.[9]

As you know, Tidewater Oil Company does business in some 80 countries around the world. As I work and travel in some of these countries, I often wonder about the secrets of economic growth.[10]

ESTABLISHING YOUR GOOD CHARACTER

The persuasiveness of a virtuous man is well known. He does not need to make a sales pitch to sell you; you will accept his advice because of your confidence in him. High on the list of important virtues are honesty, courage, patience, good temper, modesty, understanding, loyalty, consistency, and perseverance.

An old Roman, Marcus Cato, equated eloquence with "the good man skilled in speaking,"[11] contending that only a good man can qualify as a great speaker. Cicero also embraced this concept, and Quintilian, the great Roman school master, said "no man, unless he be good, can ever be an orator."[12]

We like to think that goodness is something that listeners are aware of without any mention of it. And, as G. W. Gray contends, a speaker does give off many subliminal stimuli, just below the level of perception, which reveal character, good will, and intelligence. Unaware of what they are observing, listeners will also be

[8] Lyndon B. Johnson, "The Alliance For Progress," *Vital Speeches of the Day*, **30** (June 1, 1964), p. 482.

[9] James A. Farley, "The Expanding Pattern of American Law," *Vital Speeches of the Day*, **30** (June 1, 1964), p. 497.

[10] George F. Getty II, "The Four Other Freedoms," *Vital Speeches of the Day*, **30** (June 1, 1964), p. 499.

[11] Quoted by Quintilian, *Institutes of Oratory* (Trans. John Selby Watson), Henry G. Bohn, 1856, Vol. II, p. 391.

[12] *Ibid.*, p. 392.

Fig. 5.3. Sincerity and devotion to duty won Mrs. Eleanor Roosevelt millions of admirers.

influenced by faint tension of facial muscles, slight shifts of the eyes, twitches of the mouth, subtle inflectional changes of the voice, and almost unconscious shift of the hands and body. Gray says:

What you do when you are "off guard" is often of highest significance in the estimates others make of your character; as for the subliminal stimuli, you are always "off guard." . . . The old principle handed down from ancient times, that an orator is a good man skilled in speaking, is sound from both the ethical and the psychological points of view."[13]

The best way to show your virtue is to be a good man.

You may find it necessary on occasion to make direct reference to your good character, particularly when it has been challenged, or when there may otherwise be some question about it. Notice how the following fragments reflect this aspect of ethical appeal:

> It is my honest judgment. . . .
> In all fairness, I must tell you. . . .
> I would give up my life to preserve this country.
> "You will excuse my speaking frankly because this is not a time to mince words (*Churchill*)."
> "I would fight just as hard for the poor as for the rich (*Darrow*)."

In 1951, when he was relieved from his command, Douglas MacArthur spoke in his own defense before a joint session of Congress. At this moment of tension, the much-decorated general said:

> I stand on this rostrum with a sense of deep humility and pride— humility in the weight of those great architects of our history who have stood here before me, pride in the reflection that this home of legislative debate represents human liberty in the purest form yet devised. . . .
> I do not stand here as advocate for any partisan cause. . . .
> I address you with neither rancor nor bitterness. . . .[14]

In summary, an important speaking principle is to demonstrate your good character. In his "Antidosis," Isocrates, a contemporary of Plato, explained:

> Furthermore, mark you, the man who wishes to persuade people will not be negligent as to the matter of character; no, on the contrary, he will apply himself above all to establish a most honorable name among his fellow-citizens; for who does not know that words carry greater con-

[13] Giles Wilkeson Gray and Waldo W. Braden, *Public Speaking: Principles and Practice* (2nd ed.), Harper & Row, 1963, pp. 569–572.
[14] *Congressional Record*, 1st session, 82nd Congress, Vol. 97, Pt. 3, pp. 4123–4125.

viction when spoken by men of good repute than when spoken by
men who live under a cloud, and that the argument which is made by a
man's life is of more weight than that which is furnished by words? Therefore, the stronger a man's desire to persuade his hearers, the more zeal-
ously will he strive to be honourable and to have the esteem of his
fellow-citizens.[15]

The concept of the "good man skilled in speaking" is as sound
today as it was when the principle was enunciated before the birth
of Christ.

DEMONSTRATING GOOD WILL TOWARD LISTENERS

In a remarkable speech, Kenneth I. Brown, Executive Director of
the Danforth Foundation, advises his listeners to "be men and
women with antennae," meaning of course developing a sensitivity
to the needs and wants of others. He says, "There is something
essentially tragic about the man whose armor or personality prevents
the subtle delicate shafts of human understanding that come from
another from penetrating into his own mind and heart."[16] It can be
added that it is even more "tragic" for the speaker who does not
possess these "delicate shafts of human understanding." Brown is
touching upon the very heart of ethical appeal, sometimes referred
to as "rapport," or a strong feeling of common understanding that
unites speaker and listener. It is a simple principle of human rela-
tions: You like those persons who like you.

The classic Greeks and Romans who wrote on public speaking
advised the speaker to establish with his listeners that he is a man
of good will or that he has their interests in mind in offering his
advice or proposals. You can better understand the importance of
his principle if you will consider your attitudes toward the high-
pressure salesman. Do you not resist his attempts to sell you because
you suspect him of being more interested in his commission or in
his reputation as a salesman than he is interested in your welfare?

[15] Isocrates, "Antidosis" in *The Works of Isocrates* (Trans. George Norlin),
Harvard Univ. Press, 1929, Vol. II, p. 339.
[16] Kenneth I. Brown, "Men and Women With Antennae," *Vital Speeches of
the Day*, 22 (August 15, 1956), 666–667.

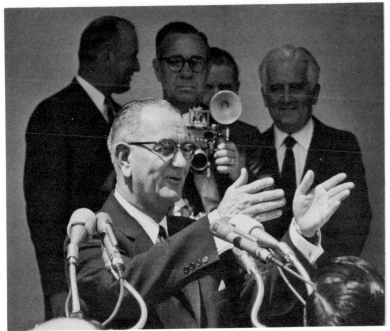

Fig. 5.4. President Lyndon Johnson shows his good will toward his listeners.

He may trap you once, but he will have more difficulty approaching you a second time.

At this moment, it seems appropriate to comment that ethical appeal like many other things is at the disposal of both good- and ill-intentioned men. On the lips of those of evil intent, ethical appeal becomes the worst type of hypocrisy and, consequently, is to be censured. However, this does not mean that ethical appeal cannot be used honestly and fairly. The sincere speaker has a duty to be a man of good will and to express it. Below are ten approaches that are sometimes employed:

1. Express respect and admiration for your listeners, their attitudes, and their activities
2. Put the interests and welfare of your listeners above your own

3. Recognize the problems and difficulties faced by the listeners
4. Signify an eagerness to help your listeners
5. Emphasize a desire to make your message clear to the listeners
6. Express admiration (even reference) for important institutions and heroes of listeners
7. Identify yourself with movements, attitudes, and programs held important by listeners
8. Avoid downgrading or criticizing what the listeners like, respect, and revere
9. Refuse to censor moral or ethical conduct of listeners
10. Put yourself on same level with listeners—be "one of the boys"

A review of the list just cited suggests that the ways to suggest good will are as numerous as are the ways to show friendship. In fact, Aristotle enumerates more than 30 ways to accomplish this objective.[17]

SOME IMPORTANT QUALITIES ASSOCIATED WITH ETHICAL APPEAL

Throughout this chapter, the implication has been that winning your way into the affection of your listeners is as much a matter of manner and attitude as it is what you actually put into the speech. In fact, *words* without the *right attitude* are empty, and seldom hit their mark. Let us consider some qualities which are closely associated with ethical appeal.

Enthusiasm

Emerson once observed, "Nothing great was ever achieved without enthusiasm."[18] The way you walk to the platform, your approach to your subject, the energy you put into your delivery—all serve to demonstrate your sincerity and your eagerness to be heard and understood. The significant speakers of our century—Winston Churchill, Franklin D. Roosevelt, John F. Kennedy, Adlai Stevenson

[17] See Aristotle, *op. cit.*, pp. 193–201.
[18] Ralph Waldo Emerson, "Circles," *Essays*, First Series, Houghton, Mifflin and Co., 1890, Vol. II, pp. 239–254.

—have had tremendous commitment and dedication to their causes. Their enthusiasm was well known and contagious.

It is interesting that Kenneth McFarland, successful popular lecturer, put enthusiasm at the top of his list of essentials for the speaker. He prefers to use the word *vitality*, saying it is "the indispensable quality" of the speaker.[19] When you hear him speak, you know that he practices what he preaches. Listeners certainly put more trust in those persons who display enthusiasm and vitality in their oral presentation.

Humor

It is difficult to know just where to fit humor into rhetorical theory, but no one will deny that the good story teller has no difficulty in opening the necessary doors to gain a hearing. For this reason the humorous incident or story is often overworked as an opening to a speech. Aristotle observed that "We . . . like those with whom we do not feel frightened or uncomfortable—nobody can like a man of whom he feels frightened."[20] The man who tells a good story disarms and puts his listeners at ease. Self-depreciating humor is excellent, for it implies that the speaker does not regard himself as superior to the listeners. Notice how Senator Margaret Chase Smith put her listeners at ease with a clever sentence:

For me to tell you [members of Overseas Press Club] of the overseas press what I saw and my impressions overseas is like Gravel Gertie telling Marilyn Monroe how to be glamorous—or Republicans telling Eisenhower how to win elections.[21]

Adlai Stevenson (a Harvard man) met the challenge of a gathering of vociferous Yale students with the following:

You know that word "egghead" is interesting. Some people think it means that you have a lot in your head, and some think it means that you have nothing on your head. In the latter respect I qualify as an egghead

[19] Kenneth McFarland, *Eloquence in Public Speaking*, Prentice Hall, 1961, pp. 238–253.
[20] Aristotle, *Rhetoric* (Trans. W. Rhys Roberts), in *The Works of Aristotle;* Oxford Univ. Press, 1946, Vol. XI, p. 1381.
[21] Margaret Chase Smith, "Impatience and Generosity," *Vital Speeches of the Day,* **XXI** (May 15, 1955), p. 1230.

Fig. 5.5. A humorous twist or anecdote may successfully relieve tension and overcome a minor crisis.

for obvious reasons. But it is when I am deemed to qualify in the former that I am happiest.[22]

When Kenneth McFarland, who is an excellent storyteller, says that "humor should be kind," he is right. For the listeners to enjoy humorous remarks, the material must not embarrass them or anyone that they greatly admire. For this reason, the story that the speaker tells about himself, his associates, or his own organization is always safer than what he may direct at someone else. Notice how Senator

[22] Adlai Stevenson A Political Speech, *The New York Times*, October 6, 1956, p. 10.

Smith and Adlai Stevenson both poked fun at themselves. It goes without saying that off-color stories or profanity can easily destroy ethos; hence, they are to be avoided.

Urge to Communicate

This quality is associated with delivery, but it is also closely related to, if not a part of, ethos. For a moment let us list some of the qualities of a speaker who really has an urge to communicate:

1. He studies his listeners carefully to learn what is necessary to communicate with them.
2. He believes intensely in his subject.
3. He prepares carefully.
4. He chooses his words with care to make sure they will carry the meaning he intends.
5. He welcomes and urges questions, and attempts to answer them to the satisfaction of his listeners.
6. He is courteous to those who interrupt him and to those with whom he is associated.
7. He stays on a point until it is understood.
8. He does not give the impression of being hurried in the development of his subject.

All of these points demonstrate the speaker's feeling of good will for his listeners and his eagerness to improve their welfare.

QUESTIONS FOR INVESTIGATION AND DISCUSSION

1. Can you judge a speaker's effectiveness by the size of the crowds he attracts? Besides speaking, what other factors attract crowds? Find some examples of speakers who attracted large crowds by their effectiveness.
2. How was "reputation" a factor in the campaign speaking in the presidential races in 1952, 1956, 1960 and 1964?
3. What is considered appropriate wearing apparel for a speaker

in your home community? What factors determine these tastes?
Compare tastes in your home community with those in your
college community.

4. How does the occasion affect the standards of appropriate
platform behavior? Give specific examples.
5. What are some substitute words or phrases for the "right to
speak"?
6. By what means can a speaker avoid seeming immodest when
he mentions his qualifications to speak on a subject?
7. What problems does a speaker encounter when he stresses his
own virtues? Are there occasions and situations in which a
display of virtues is invited and encouraged?
8. What are subliminal and supraliminal stimuli? How are these
important to speaker? What control do you have over these
stimuli?
9. Under what conditions "will truth prevail"? Consider this
sentence from Aristotle's *Rhetoric:* "Truth and justice are by
nature more powerful than their opposites."
10. Does the *effective* speaker have to be a *good* man? What are
the differences between the "good" (ethical) and the effective
speaker? Consult several textbooks on this question; for example,
see James McBurney and Ernest Wrage, *The Art of Good
Speech,* Prentice-Hall, 1953.
11. Is it necessary for an ethical person to include ethical appeal
in a speech? Explain.
12. How does the high-pressure salesman fail to communicate his
good will? What is meant by "low-pressure selling"? If possible,
investigate these phrases in some books on salesmanship. How
are these concepts related to showing good will?
13. If you follow the suggestions for showing good will given on
pages 101–102 are you insincere? Under what circumstances?
How are these techniques sometimes used by demagogues?
14. How is humor associated with ethos? Under what circumstances
would humor actually weaken your ethos with your listeners?
15. In addition to those qualities discussed in the chapter, what are
some other important qualities associated with ethos? For

example, consult Clinton Rossiter's *The American Presidency* (rev. ed.), The New American Library, 1960, chap. 5. What qualities does Rossiter associate with the presidency which apply to ethos? Which would not generally build ethos?

16. How is ethos or ethical appeal related to ethics?
17. Would the ethos which was effective with an American audience be effective with a Japanese audience? A Russian audience?

ASSIGNMENTS

SPEAKING ASSIGNMENTS

1. Report on how a speaker whom you have heard recently in a face-to-face situation used ethical appeal. If possible, have several members of the class evaluate the same speech and make independent evaluations. Then compare your conclusions.

2. Deliver a two-minute speech of introduction for some distinguished person. Attempt to build up his intelligence, good character and good will.

RESEARCH ASSIGNMENT

Investigate what the classical writers, Aristotle, Cicero, and Quintilian, have to say about ethical appeal. See Lester Thonssen, editor, *Selected Readings in Rhetoric and Public Speaking* (H. W. Wilson Co., 1942).

WRITTEN ASSIGNMENT

Prepare a written analysis of the *ethos* in a recent speech found in the daily newspapers, or in *Vital Speeches of the Day.* For help on setting up standards consult Lester Thonssen and A. Craig Baird, *Speech Criticism*, Ronald, 1948, chap. 13.

BULLETIN BOARD ASSIGNMENT

Theme: Prominent American Political Speakers.

SUGGESTED READINGS

Braden, Waldo W., and Mary Louise Gehring, *Speech Practices: A Resource Book for the Student of Public Speaking,* Harper & Row, 1958, chap. 4.

Crocker, Lionel, *Public Speaking for College Students* (3rd ed.), American Book, 1956, chap. 3.

Freely, Austin J., "*Ethos,* Eisenhower, and the 1956 Campaign," *Central States Speech Journal,* IX (Spring, 1958), 24–26.

Pross, Edward L., "Practical Implications of the Aristotelian Concept of Ethos," *Southern Speech Journal,* XVII (May, 1952), 257–264.

Thonssen, Lester (Ed.), *Selected Readings in Rhetoric and Public Speaking,* H. W. Wilson, 1942.

Sattler, William M., "Conceptions of Ethos in Ancient Rhetoric," *Speech Monographs,* XIV (1947), 55–65.

Walter, Otis, "What You, Speaks So Loud. . . . ," *Today's Speech,* III (April, 1955), 3–6.

VI

EFFECTIVE DELIVERY

The primary goal in speaking is the communication of the message to listeners. That is the foremost goal, nothing else. You must direct all aspects of the process toward contributing meaning and power to what you say. Albert J. Beveridge hit this point hard: "Whenever a speaker fails to make his audience forget voice, gesture, and even the speaker himself, whenever he fails to make the listeners conscious only of the living truth he utters, he has failed in his speech itself. . . ."[1]

---

[1] Albert J. Beveridge, "Public Speaking," in Ashley H. Thorndike (Ed.), *Modern Eloquence,* Modern Eloquence Corporation, 1923, Vol. I, xxxviii.

Fig. 6.1. Governor Romney's gestures are characteristic of his delivery and convey the spirit behind his ideas. Gestures and mannerisms which are artificial or contrived detract from a point being developed.

The principle is simple: As long as the listeners are attending to the unfolding of the thought, you are succeeding; but when they focus upon what you are doing or how you are saying it, you are failing. When you are effective, you can expect your listeners to feel, "I understand," "I know what you are driving at," "I believe you;" but when you stimulate in them such impressions as "what superb gestures," "how handsome he was," "what a beautiful voice," "what poise and grace," you have emphasized yourself instead of your message. Richard Whately summarized this as follows: "When delivery is really good the hearers . . . never think about it, but are exclusively occupied with the sense it conveys and the feeling it excites."[2]

In other words, when you keep attention on what you are saying—not on what you are doing—your delivery is excellent.

[2] Richard Whately, *Element of Rhetoric* (7th ed.), John W. Parker, 1851, p. 231.

THREE REQUISITES OF GOOD DELIVERY

There are basically three requisites to an effective delivery:

1. *Contributes to the Message.* Gestures, facial expression, movement, posture, and voice control should add a dimension of meaning not present on the printed page. Effective delivery provides the highlights and shadows, and it will help fasten your ideas with the listeners.

2. *Appropriate to the Speaking Environment.* You must adapt your vocal projection and bodily movement to the physical demands of the time and place of the speech. When speaking to a meeting out-of-doors, you must use larger movements and a louder voice than when you speak in a small room which calls for a quiet, subdued manner.

3. *Represents the Speaker Well.* Your delivery must fit your physical attributes and personality as well as your abilities. Through your voice and action you gain acceptance, hold interest, and achieve your goal. Not hearing what you say, your listeners may form their opinions on the basis of a superficial observation of an unfortunate mannerism or a voice break.

CONTROL OF BODILY ACTIVITY

Approach to the Platform

When your turn to speak comes, have in hand any materials that you intend to use: notes, handouts, visual aids. Walk to the center of the platform or speaking area with confidence and quiet dignity. Do not start your remarks while you are still walking to your place. Keep away from the edge of the platform or the front row of chairs. Once in position, pause a moment to permit the listeners to focus upon you and to prepare to listen. By your manner and facial expression, create the impression that you have something important to say.

Both photos, Homer Page, Ford Foundation

Fig. 6.2. Vocal projection and bodily movement must be adapted to the physical demands of the time, place, and mood of the particular speaking environment, and must fit your own physical and personality attributes as well. Contrast the requirements for these two speaking situations!

After uttering your last sentence, look a moment at your listeners, and then walk to your seat with quiet dignity. Students often ask whether they should thank the audience for listening. This custom, once good etiquette, is no longer considered necessary.

SUMMARY OF DISTRACTING MANNERISMS

The previous section suggested many things to avoid. They centered around mannerisms that detract from what you have to say. Below is a summary of twenty-five of these annoying habits of the beginning speaker.

1. Wringing hands
2. Rolling or playing with notes
3. Jingling money or keys
4. Buttoning and unbuttoning coat
5. Pulling an ear or a nose
6. Fumbling with a pencil
7. Putting thumbs under belt
8. Standing with hands on hips
9. Scratching
10. Fussing with ring, watch, or beads
11. Fixing tie or pin
12. Clutching or straightening clothing
13. Cracking knuckles
14. Looking at the ceiling or out the window
15. Shifting eyes constantly from place to place
16. Folding and unfolding arms
17. Giving nervous or silly laugh
18. Standing with feet too wide apart or close together
19. Rocking backward and forward from heels to toes
20. Standing cross-legged
21. Shifting constantly from one foot to the other
22. Placing foot on a chair or table
23. Leaning heavily on a lectern or reading stand
24. Wetting lips frequently
25. Smoothing repeatedly or replacing stray wisps of hair

DISTRACTING MANNERISMS

Looking at Floor

Leaning on Table

Awkward Stance

Playing with Beads

Fig. 6.5. Four examples of distracting mannerisms. The stance illustrated in the *upper left* may be comfortably casual in other situations, but is an important don't for public-speaking, as is the awkward hands-on-hips attitude of the figure at *bottom right*. Gazing at the floor (*upper right*) and fingering beads or other irrelevant objects only draws your listeners' attention away from the speech.

THE VOICE

In the first chapter of the book, we considered what a speech is, suggesting that to qualify in this category a discourse must be heard and understood. This concept puts the vocal aspects of delivery at the very center of effective speechmaking. The production and control of voice is a most complex process about which much could be said. It may surprise you to learn that there is no specific vocal mechanism; voice is an *overlaid* function; that is, it uses structures with more basic functions, i.e., the lungs to breathe, the tongue to taste, the teeth to chew.

The goal of this section is not to tell you how to develop a beautiful voice or to tell you what to do if you have something seriously wrong with your voice. Both objectives are important, but they deserve more space and attention than we can give here.

But one word of advice: Before you decide to change your voice or conclude that you have some serious problem, *you should consult an expert.*

Below are presented certain minimum essentials well within the reach of any normal person. If you meet these goals, you can communicate effectively.

Strive To Be Understood

If you have attended a football or basketball game recently, you have had convincing proof that the human voice is capable of great volume and can take considerable punishment without being seriously damaged. The worst that happens to voices of most sports fans is slight hoarseness which soon clears up. The average person does not need a technical explanation as to how to amplify his volume, how to be heard; he simply increases the energy to speak louder.

Distinctness involves matters of articulation. The carrying power of voice is in the vowel sounds; the intelligibility of speech is mainly a matter of the distinctness of consonants. "For speech that can easily be understood for any distance, therefore, you must attend to both your vowels and your consonants—in other words, to your entire utterance."[5] Attempt to give a certain crispness to your word formation. Use your tongue and lips and other vocal organs vigorously. Don't drop those final consonants, and don't drop out any sounds.

Being heard and understood starts with an urge to communicate. The person who is eager to communicate is alert to signs that his listeners may not be hearing what he is saying. When you are in doubt, you can insert the question "Can you hear what I am saying?" as a check on yourself. Feedback in the form of puzzled expressions, restlessness, and disinterest should suggest that you must try a little harder to project what you are saying out to that very back row.

Sometimes women who have repeatedly been told since childhood that they must be ladylike have difficulty projecting their voices. When they are asked "to speak up"—perhaps loud enough to be heard in an average sized classroom—they complain that they "feel like" they are "shouting." Such persons (this also includes some men) need to develop an awareness for what is adequate projection.

Men with particularly deep voices also have difficulty being understood. In the Lincoln-Douglas debates of 1858, Lincoln with his sharp, rather shrill, unmusical voice was heard at the edges of the crowds. When he appeared at Cooper Union it is reported that he spoke "in high-keyed voice that could be heard distinctly in the farthermost corner of the big auditorium."[6] On the other hand, the deep voice of Stephen A. Douglas was not always understood.

Intelligibility is difficult when you attempt to speak with something in your mouth. Remember speech is an overlaid function. To talk with chewing gum, a cigar, a cigarette, or a pipe in your mouth is likely to result in a muffled quality. The gum-chewing speaker is under a distinct handicap.

Use a Conversational Approach

Wendell Phillips, fiery agitator and superb speaker of the nineteenth century, became known for his unusual ability to stir his hearers. But he never fitted the stereotype that many persons had of a man who was always in the midst of controversy. The curious people who came to jeer were dismayed by his quiet com-

[5] Gray and Braden, *op. cit.*, p. 548.
[6] William E. Barton, *President Lincoln*, Bobbs-Merrill, 1953, Vol. I, 73.

posure. Much of his charm resulted from a conversational approach to his listeners. One observer said of him:

> The character of the voice—the man in it—had the effect of "finding" its auditor. It had an *intimate* tone, as if it were speaking to each one as an unknown friend. . . . His public speaking was his part of a public conversation addressed, as it were, to the farthest auditor. . . .[7]

On this point, Phillips is worth emulating. The successful speaker tries to break down barriers through using the enlarged conversational approach; this means that he attempts to talk to listeners in the same manner as he does in earnest conversation. Of course, in a large auditorium or in an intensely emotional environment, the speaker amplifies and extends his vocal power, but his model remains the same.

It is not uncommon for the novice to opine, more or less seriously, that he wants to "sound like a speaker" or still better to "be an orator." In love with the ring of his own voice, he gives forth in the way he imagines Patrick Henry or Daniel Webster must have sounded. Such is the case of young ministers, who imitate country preachers and drift into a ministerial pattern or what Whately called "a pompous spout or modulated whine."[8] It is evident that these high-schoolish "orators" draw attention to themselves instead of to their remarks.

The conversational speaker attempts to radiate friendliness, good will, and reassurance. The public-address system, radio, and television have put a great premium upon this type of naturalness. Achieving the same rapport is even more difficult when using a manuscript, but reading is no different from speaking.

Watch Your Rate

The fast talker fits the stereotype of the high-pressure salesman. Listeners often distrust or feel uneasy with his mile-a-minute talker because they suspect that he wishes to avoid questions and to gain acceptance without thoughtful analysis. The woman who speaks

---

[7] Anonymous, quoted by Willard Hayes Yeager, "Wendell Phillips," in William N. Brigance (Ed.), *A History and Criticism of American Public Address*, McGraw-Hill, 1944, Vol. I, 359–360.

[8] Whately, *op. cit.*, p. 239.

too rapidly is referred to as a "chatterbox," meaning that she is long on talk and low on thought content. The slow drawl may suggest the country bumpkin. It is evident that speech rate is associated with many uncomplimentary images.

How fast should you speak? Of course, rate of speech is a personality characteristic differing from individual to individual. Franklin D. Roosevelt spoke at a rate of about 105 to 110 words per minute, a comparatively slow pace for an American male. Most effective speakers stay within the range of 140 to 175 words per minute.

It is a comparatively simple matter to check your rate. Simply count out 100 or 200 words and time your reading of the passage. Or, if you have a tape recorder, you can check your extemporaneous rate. When you are speaking from manuscript, estimate reading time by simply dividing your rate per minute into your total words. In five minutes you should be able to deliver about a 750 word speech or not much more than three double-spaced pages of typed material.

Avoid Meaningless Vocalization

Fluency is taken as a sign of being well prepared and knowing what you are talking about. The hesitant speaker is difficult to listen to and may be considered as one who has something to hide. The insertion in your remarks of "and-a's," "uh's," and other meaningless vocalizations makes comprehension difficult because the listener soon finds himself concentrating on your idiosyncrasies instead of what you are saying. Likewise, frequent repetition of pet phrases, such as "on the other hand," "and stuff like that," "you know," "don't you know," is also distracting. The only way to eliminate the vocal mannerisms is to have them forcefully called to your attention.

Take Advantage of Changes of Pace

There are dead-pan voices as well as dead-pan faces. Activity, change, flexibility, and variety add interest to any presentation. Monotony, lackadaisicalness, and motionlessness will put an audience to sleep. Listeners soon tire of a speaker who drones on at the same rate, same intensity, and same patterns. The secret to stirring interest is change of pace; that is, variations in (1) pitch, (2) emphasis, (3) loudness, and (4) time.

Fig. 6.6. Edward P. Morgan, ABC news commentator, is famous for his easy conversational approach to news broadcasting.

Many of the newscasters on radio and television—such as Chet Huntley, John Daly, and Walter Cronkite—are masters of the change of pace. Their voices determine their value to a network. Those who remember Edward R. Murrow will recall how he achieved what Reynolds and Thonssen called "a personal type of punctuation supplied by changes in time, inflection, and stress." They continue:

A distinctive feature of his delivery is what he called "unorthodox timing." It commands attention from the very beginning: "This [pause] is London" or "This [pause] is the news. . . ."
Murrow is adept at controlling inflectional variation. The inflectional changes are used effectively to reinforce ideas. They are also used in a subtler way, but with equal incisiveness and precision, to convey im-

pressions which, if expressed in words, would clearly amount to open editorializing and persuasion. Indeed, objective analysis may with skillful vocal manipulation become charged with advocacy.[9]

Let us enumerate some ways to achieve change of pace:

1. Use a soft (or low) voice to indicate that you are giving the listener confidential material
2. Give an important phrase or sentence in low or high key to indicate importance
3. Give important material at a slower rate (Is—this—a dagger—I see—before—me?)
4. Indicate rapid movement by increasing your tempo and using staccato tones
5. Pause before or after an important word or revelation of important information
6. Pause to give the listeners an opportunity to catch up or to relax
7. Increase tempo as you reach a climax

Present Yourself Favorably

You have a distinctive quality or timbre which identifies you. Voice is the trademark of radio and television personalities, such as Lowell Thomas who is known to millions of Americans by his sharp, penetrating voice.

Of course, voices vary in quality, and some persons are more fortunate than others in native endowment, but voices can be cultivated through hours of well-planned practice.

Some of the common faults of voice are (1) nasal, (2) husky, (3) thin, (4)strident, and (5) breathy. It is recommended that the person who develops any of these qualities, or any other serious vocal problem, seek the advice of an expert and that he not attempt changing his voice without professional advice.

Within your range of potentialities you can win a favorable hearing. Your voice will reflect your attitudes. If, inside, you are eager to communicate, and you like or respect your listeners, your voice will probably carry though in expressing these same attitudes.

[9] Ota Thomas Reynolds and Lester Thonssen, "The Reporter as Orator: Edward R. Murrow," Loren Reid (Ed.), *American Public Address*, Univ. of Missouri Press, 1961, p. 329.

Fierce determination

Driving home a point

Illustrative explanation

Dramatic expansion

Fig. 6.7. Walter Reuther demonstrates effective changes of pace.

Quiet, reasonable appeal

Whately recommends that the speaker withdraw his thought from the voice and "dwell as intently as possible on the Sense, trusting to nature to suggest spontaneously the proper emphasis and tones."[10] Good advice if not carried too far.

Listen to a recording of your voice. What you hear approximates what your listeners will hear. If you do not like what you hear, try projecting a pleasant attitude. Experiment with what you can reflect through your voice quality.

QUESTIONS FOR INVESTIGATION AND DISCUSSION

1. What is considered effective delivery in your home community? Does this standard vary from the standard presented in this chapter? If it does, please attempt to discover why there is this difference.
2. Are there different standards of delivery for different professions and groups? In other words, is the minister in your church expected to use a delivery which would not be acceptable elsewhere? Why (or why not) is this true?
3. Have styles of delivery changed? If possible, find descriptions of some of the great orators of the past; namely, Webster, Lincoln, Phillips, Ingersoll, Bryan, Wilson, and F. D. Roosevelt.
4. What effect have radio and television had on delivery?
5. What is implied in the word "naturalness" in delivery? Does *naturalness* mean *habitual*? Should the country bumpkin, tomboy, or effeminate boy be natural in delivery?
6. When is naturalness a handicap?
7. Does a speaker need "tension" to be an effective speaker? Is tension essential to effectiveness? When? Under what condition? What kind of tension?
8. What is good posture? Demonstrate.
9. How is delivery an aspect of speaking style in the way language choice is?

[10] Whately, *op. cit.*, p. 229.

10. What are some of the attributes of voice which affect the meaning of words?
11. How does delivery add a dimension to meaning which cannot be found on the printed page?
12. What is the relationship of voice and personality?
13. How do you explain the sentence, "The carrying power of a voice is in the vowel sounds"?
14. Why does a higher-pitched voice carry better than a low voice?
15. What is the meaning of the sentence, "Speech is an overlaid function"? See Giles Wilkeson Gray and Claude M. Wise, *The Bases of Speech* (3rd ed.), Harper & Row, 1959, pp. 476–478.

ASSIGNMENTS

CLASS PROJECT

In this and the last three chapters of this textbook, assignments are a planned series of speeches. The completion of the assignment in the present chapter prepares the class for the assignment in Chapter VIII.

The instructor, or a committee from the class, will select for investigation four or five themes such as civil rights, health insurance, the mass media, federal aid to education, or other topics of current interest. (The annual collegiate and high-school debate propositions are excellent for this purpose.) The class as a whole may select a single theme for concentrated study or the class may be divided into groups of five to seven, with each pursuing a different topic.

1. The *research* may be limited to a common source book such as a number of the *Reference Shelf Series* (H. W. Wilson Co.), *Goals for Americans, The Report of the President's Commission on National Goals* (Prentice-Hall, 1960), the current issue of the *NUEA Debate Handbook*, Herbert W. Hildebrandt's *Issues of Our Times* (Macmillan, 1963), or Carroll C. Arnold and others, *The Speaker's Resource Book* (Scott Foresman and Co., 1961), Edwin Black and Harry P. Kerr, *American Issues: A Sourcebook for Speech Topics* (Harcourt, Brace & World, 1961). The project may also include the following:

a. Assemble a class or group scrapbook of clippings on the theme. Each member is responsible for pertinent articles, but each week a different student can serve as custodian, mounting and labeling the clippings in the group scrapbook.

b. Some members may contact pressure groups and professional organizations for free pamphlet material (see pp. 29–30).

c. Some groups will find it useful to prepare a cooperative bibliography of available materials in current periodicals.

2. For the *first speaking assignment,* each member will prepare a five-minute speech of exploration of an aspect of the general theme. You may pursue one of the following:

a. A definition of confusing terms or concepts in theme

b. Analysis of the cause for discussion; why is theme timely

c. History of an aspect of theme, earlier systems, felt needs, agitations for, etc.

For symposium groups: If class is divided into groups with each considering a different topic, each group will have a class period for its presentation. The group should use about thirty minutes for its presentation and ten minutes for questions.

PERFORMANCE ASSIGNMENTS

1. Describe by *pantomime only* some event or process: Tell a story, play one hole of a golf game, shine your shoes, make a cake, get breakfast (as in the play "Our Town"), etc.

2. Characterize a well-known campus or community character by your walk, posture, and voice. Have members of the class identify the person.

3. Divide the class into pairs for rehearsal. Each member of the class will deliver his speech to his partner before he delivers to the class. In these practice sessions work on eliminating mannerisms.

4. Record your speech and make a careful study of your vocal quality. Do you demonstrate the qualities listed on pages 119–126?

5. Find illustrations from living speakers (perhaps class members) for each of the five qualities mentioned on page 129.

6. Rate the delivery of each member of the class on the following:

	Poor	Fair	Average	Excellent	Superior
Naturalness					
Variety					
Animation					
Purposefulness					
Pleasingness					

Total _____

WRITTEN ASSIGNMENTS

Write a speech biography in which you analyze your own assets and liabilities as a speaker. Consider such questions as the following, insofar as they apply:

1. Why I enrolled in a public speaking course. (If it is required, state the probable reasons why it is required in your curriculum.)
2. What I hope to accomplish as a result of taking the course.
3. The kind of speaker I should like to be.
4. The social and professional uses to which I may put my ability in speaking.
5. Any pleasant or unpleasant experiences I may have had as a speaker.
6. My present recognized faults in speaking.
7. Difficulties in speaking that I hope to overcome.

SPEAKING ASSIGNMENTS

1. Deliver a five-minute speech on one of the following topics:

a. How naturalness caused a speaker to fail.
b. How poor voice control caused a speaker to fail.
c. How superb delivery saved the day.
d. My ideal speaker (in terms of delivery, of course).

2. Give a talk on some subject that touches the everyday affairs of your listeners. Get as close to the front row as you conveniently

can, and try to get a direct reaction from the audience. You may address specific questions to individual members, asking for additional information, for verification, for opinion, etc. Establish as high a degree of *rapport* through your manner of presentation as you can.

SUGGESTED READINGS

Crocker, Lionel, *Public Speaking for College Students* (3rd ed.), American Book, 1956, chap. 4.

Gray, Giles W., and Waldo W. Braden, *Public Speaking: Principles and Practice* (2nd ed.), Harper and Row, 1963, chaps. 6, 28, and 29.

Gray, Giles Wilkeson, and Claude Merton Wise, *The Bases of Speech* (3rd ed.), Harper & Row, 1959.

Hargis, Donald E., "Some Basic Considerations in Teaching Voice," *Speech Teacher*, **XII** (September, 1963) 214–218.

Kenyon, John S., and Thomas Knott, *A Pronouncing Dictionary of American English*, Merriam, 1949.

Parrish, W. M., "The Concept of 'Naturalness'," *Quarterly Journal of Speech*, **XXXVII** (December, 1951), 448–454.

Weaver, Andrew Thomas, and Ordean Gerhard Ness, *The Fundamentals and Forms of Speech* (rev. ed.), Odyssey, 1963, chap. 6.

Weaver, Carl H., "Don't Look It Up—Listen!" *Speech Teacher*, **VI** (September, 1957), 240–246.

Wise, Claude Merton, *Applied Phonetics*, Prentice-Hall, 1957.

❖❖❖ VII

YOUR PRONUNCIATION[1]

DOES PRONUNCIATION MATTER?

Although your pronunciation is less important than your thought, it can nevertheless be an obstacle or impediment to your communication of that thought if it is either unclear or inappropriate.

Unclear pronunciation increases the difficulty your audience has in understanding what you are trying to communicate. If you refer to a "martyr" as a "mortar," or to "power" as "par," declare an issue to be "irrevelant" rather than "irrelevant" or confuse "council" with

[1] This chapter was prepared by Francine Merritt, Associate Professor of Speech, Louisiana State University.

131

Fig. 7.1 Substandard or slovenly pronunciation can spoil an otherwise effective speech. The difference between good and poor pronunciation sometimes rests on a subtle distinction.

"consul"; if you substitute "ax" for "acts," you compel your audience to expend some of its mental energy on contextual analysis to determine the appropriate words. Even complete misunderstanding is possible: A comedy of errors has been known to occur in a conversation in which one person inquired about a missing "cord" and the other understood the item to be a "card." And all of us come to know the embarrassment resulting from indistinct pronunciation of proper names for social introductions. Any speaker can and should eliminate the handicap that unclear pronunciation presents to his audience.

Inappropriate pronunciation, though it seldom presents a serious problem in understanding, can be compared with incorrect spelling. Just as you will find it advantageous to observe the conventions of spelling expected by the recipient of your business letter, so you will find it desirable to use pronunciations acceptable to the best educated segment of your audience. Inappropriate pronunciation can make the audience question your competence as a speaker—your experience, knowledge, education. An audience expects no faltering when a chemist pronounces the names of his compounds, a theatre critic the names of playwrights, a minister Biblical names, an announcer the titles of musical compositions, a doctor his medical terms. And an audience finds it difficult to credit a speaker with valuable ideas when his pronunciation—which they take to be indicative of his education—is open to criticism. Like a poorly spelled letter, a speech transmitted in poorly pronounced language is subject to undervaluation. If you want your ideas to receive the favorable attention they deserve, you will make your pronunciation speak well of you.

IS GOOD PRONUNCIATION DIFFICULT TO ACHIEVE?

Pronunciation, like spelling, is based on convention and the usage of the educated, cultured portion of society, the "prestige group" of the community. Pronunciation problems—that is, deviations from convention and usage by this group—occur with words in three different categories: everyday words, unfamiliar words, and proper names or foreign words.

Everyday Words

In our early years, we acquire our pronunciations as we do our vocabulary and grammar, by imitation of those whom we hear—our family and friends. "Family mispronunciations" are perpetuated in this way, as when, for example, in a community accustomed to another pronunciation, all the members of one family say "putt" for "put." More commonly, mispronunciations are community-wide or are prevalent in even larger geographical areas. These are the most difficult of all pronunciation errors to eradicate because, first, they occur in the simplest, most ordinary words (words like *egg, dance, ask, lost, gone, want, oil, send,* and *can't*), and second, good models of such words are often difficult to find in the immediate environment. Worse still, you can almost never eliminate errors of this type by consulting a dictionary. Instead you must have some type of "ear training," that is, exposure to large amounts of oral language pronounced well. Real improvement may even require enrollment in a class in speech improvement or individual attention from a coach of voice and diction. Short of these measures, you can train yourself to more discriminating listening habits if you will use as models the radio and television announcers heard on national networks. The next step is to imitate deliberately the pronunciations obviously different from your own.

Some words of caution about this imitative procedure are in order. Reliance on the speech of another for a model has its dangers. Let us suppose you recognize a pronunciation different from your own. The dissimilarity may indicate that your pronunciation is inferior, but, again, it may be merely a reflection of certain generally acceptable regional differences. You may require several models before electing to change your pronunciations.

Merely listening and recognizing differences will not improve your own speech greatly. To improve your pronunciation of familiar words like *get, just,* and *catch,* you must change your old habits of speech through oral practice even while you continue to be exposed to familiar mispronunciations. A tape recorder on which you record both your model's speaking and your own attempts at imitation and improvement will assist your practice periods. However much you may want to improve, only intent self-analysis and persistent practice on specific problems can bring significant improvement to your pronunciation of everyday words.

Unfamiliar Words

Words of whose pronunciations you are doubtful probably come from outside your normal speaking vocabulary. Generally you meet them first in print, but eventually you must pronounce them. If you rely on guesswork rather than consult a dictionary, you are likely to err in pronouncing words like *prelate, façade,* or *extrapolate* unless you have heard them. A good dictionary should solve your

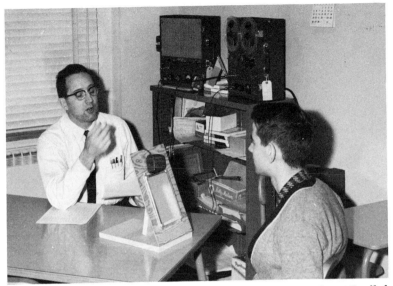

Fig. 7.2. Tape recording sessions provide an excellent way to study your diction and to compare your pronunciation with that of a model.

problem. Unfortunately some of us are unable to use a dictionary successfully, even though we have been encouraged to consult it in school. The reasons for our difficulty with unfamiliar words become apparent when we examine written and spoken English.

First, English pronunciation and spelling are inconsistent with themselves and with one another. Many who pronounce badly are also poor spellers. Both speakers and spellers depend on analogy for assistance. Yet even the simplest English words, as *one* and *who* readily demonstrate, are sufficiently irregular in pronunciation when compared with their spelling to prove that analogy is often unreliable. By the time he begins to read well, a child has learned that *some* and *home* must not be allowed to rhyme in spite of appearances, but the adult who refers to British politics must learn to avoid analogy in pronouncing the name Douglas-Home. Whether analogy assists or handicaps the speaker who must pronounce *hearth* depends on whether he happens to think of it as analogous with *heart, earth,* or *heath.* When polysyllables occur, the speaker who depends on analogy sometimes resorts to division of words into recognizable parts. Such a practice produces for *solace, ribald,* and *primate* the pronunciations *so-lace, ri-bald,* and *prim-ate,* all likely to distress discriminating listeners.

Second, even the consistencies of English are not widely known. English has a complex history that, if known, would be helpful. More than half of our English words are derived from French or Latin. At many different periods in history, English has borrowed widely from different languages to add vocabulary to its basic Old English (Germanic) foundation. For this reason, words that appear to resemble one another in spelling may vary widely in pronunciation and vice versa. Yet seeming inconsistencies can be accounted for if the history of the language is known. For example, the last syllables of *courage* and *garage,* both borrowed from French, do not resemble one another in sound, although the spellings are like, because *courage* entered the English vocabulary quite early and developed characteristics of pronunciation that *garage,* particularly the American pronunciation, has not had time to attain. (Compare *mirage, barrage, adage, visage, roughage,* and *postage.*) One might say that borrowed words remain foreign for a time, then become naturalized, and eventually are treated as if they were native Anglo-Saxon words, changing pronunciation with each step. But to use this pattern of change in English pronunciation to advantage usually requires more extensive knowledge than many of us can bring to bear.

Third, the nature of English rhythm and its influence on pronunciation are not widely understood. English, particularly in the United States, appears to have what might be called a rocking-horse rhythm; that is, it prefers to alternate syllables of greater and lesser stress and to reject adjacent syllables of equal stress. This tendency toward alternating degrees of stress in American English makes syllabic stress unstable and leads unwary speakers to accent polysyllables inappropriately at times, e.g., *comparable* becomes *comPARable.* Word groups can be similarly affected, so that the phrase *the Supreme Court* becomes, in appropriate rocking-horse style, the *SUpreme COURT.* Some of the acceptable alternate pronunciations only now receiving dictionary sanction are the products of just such pressures. (Compare the different pronunciations of *disputant, dictionary, cerebrum,* etc.)

Fourth, helpful spelling, when it does occur, is often ignored. In fact, there appears to be a direct relationship between poor spelling and poor pronunciation, especially when a letter or sound is omitted, inserted, or reversed. A close look at the spelling of *larynx* (not larnyx), *pharynx, length* (not lenth), *strength, athlete* (not athalete), *athletic, pronunciation* (not pronounciation), *perform* (not preform), *similar* (not simular), etc., should provide you with visual clues for improved pronunciation of these frequently distorted words.

To summarize, guesswork and analogy are unreliable and spelling is inconsistent as a guide to pronunciation. American English rhythm sometimes encourages inappropriate pronunciation. And the assistance that the history of the English language could give is not readily available to many. The best solution to the speaker's problem of pronouncing unfamiliar words is the acquisition and consistent use of a good dictionary.

Proper Names and Foreign Words

Words in these categories are often deceptive. Cities of the same name are not pronounced alike: Lima, Peru, and Lima, Ohio; Cairo, Egypt, and Cairo, Illinois. Proper names originally pronounced the same are now sometimes like, sometimes unlike: Hayden and Haydn, Mayor and Meyer, etc. Any speaker has occasion to pronounce strange American geographical names: Waxahatchie, Ouachita, Des Moines, Wichita, Okeechobee, Sault Sainte Marie, Mexia, Nacogdoches, Natchitoches, etc. And to be judged an educated person, a speaker must be able to pronounce appropriately, if need arises, a great variety of foreign and American proper names: Mozart, Chopin, Goethe, Millet, Ingres, Rodin, Inge, Ciardi, Sapir, Wundt, Sukarno, Tshombe.

Unlike other words, proper names and foreign phrases are non-conforming, following few familiar rules. One general principle applicable to proper names of people and places in the United States is this: A person has the right to determine the pronunciation of his own name, and a place is called what its residents wish it to be named, despite the spelling. This principle will lead to considerable indecision when you must call a roll of unfamiliar names. It also leads to increased need for geographical dictionaries and handbooks that indicate local pronunciations of the names of towns, rivers, counties, and mountains.

Some foreign names and phrases retain much of their original pronunciation when they are spoken by Americans: *Nazi, pizza, faux pas.* Others are "anglicized"; that is, they are pronounced as though they were of English origin without reference to their derivation: *Caesar, sine die, status quo.* Latin phrases in common use occasionally have two acceptable pronunciations, one resembling Latin, the other modified English, as is the case with *alma mater.*

REFERENCE BOOKS TO AID PRONUNCIATION

At least one good dictionary is indispensable. Its value is measured by its completeness, its quality of scholarship, and the recency of its revision. The more words it contains, common and proper, native and foreign-derived, the greater is its potential usefulness to you. However, regardless of its size, the qualifications of its contributors determine its real value. Superior (i.e., authoritative) dictionaries are produced by large editorial boards of linguists, each of whom is a specialist in some aspect of language. Such dictionaries are not to be compared with a word book prepared by one person (sometimes unidentified) and sold in a supermarket for 98¢. Reputable dictionaries are also regularly updated to include new words as well as new meanings and pronunciations for established words.

No single dictionary can possibly contain every word that you may need to check. However, you have available the resources of school and community libraries containing geographical, biographical, and classical dictionaries, literary handbooks, pronouncing manuals, dictionaries for broadcasters, etc.

Learning the Use of Dictionaries

Since many who consult dictionaries for pronunciations find themselves unable to interpret the information they have found, you may welcome some suggestions.

First learn to use your own dictionary effectively. *Read aloud* carefully the preliminary directions for its use, commonly found in the foreword, introduction, or guide to pronunciation. Selecting at

Louisiana State University

Fig. 7.3. When you study pronunciation, there is no substitute for oral practice.

random some pages of words to pronounce, practice interpreting the symbols by which the sounds are represented for both the words you know and the unfamiliar words. When you are studying pronunication, *always practice aloud.*

Once you have developed ease in your use of one dictionary, turn to others to familiarize yourself with them. Dictionaries are not alike. Using them carelessly without regard to their individual differences will lead to misinterpretation of their information. All dictionaries use one or some combination of three different systems of representing sounds: respelling, diacritical marking, and phonetic symbolization. None of these are uniform from dictionary to dictionary. Respelling relies on the possibility of finding a group of ordinary spelling letters that will represent pronunciation without ambiguity, e.g., *chic* is pronounced "sheek." Diacritical marks are symbols added to the spelling of a word to indicate which of the potential sounds of a spelling letter is actually to be used. The meaning of each diacritical mark for each letter is indicated by the use of a "key word," which is presumed to be pronounced correctly by the user of the dictionary. Most dictionaries use a combination of respelling and diacritical markings, since neither is entirely satisfactory alone.

Phonetic symbols, the third method of indicating pronunciation, usually require special training for the user, because they include unorthodox symbols unlike spelling letters and because auditory training is essential for accurate interpretation of the symbols. However, an occasional phonetic symbol—most often the schwa [ə]—finds its way into other dictionaries.

Unfortunately, there is no perfect method of showing sounds to the eye, and none of these methods or combinations of methods of representating sounds are entirely standardized. Some pronunciations cannot be shown by respelling. Diacritical marks are not uniform from dictionary to dictionary, though many are duplicated. Even the dictionaries using phonetic symbolization have important variations, as a comparison of Kenyon and Knott's *A Pronouncing Dictionary of American English* and Daniel Jones's *An English Pronouncing Dictionary* will show.

Since the use of phonetic dictionaries requires special oral instruction and since dictionaries with respelling and diacritical marks are more readily available, you should train yourself to convert respelling and diacritical marks into appropriate speech sounds. You will be fortunate if you have an opportunity to learn phonetic symbols. Meantime here are a few helpful facts about the more common dictionaries:

The *macron*, or "long mark," over any vowel letter indicates that you should say the *name* of that letter; e.g., the first vowel sound in *mācron* is the same sound as the name of the first letter of the alphabet, *a*.

The *breve*, or "short mark," over any vowel letter indicates the sound represented in most short syllables like these: *bĭt, bĕt, băt, gŏt, bŭt.*

Although the phonetic symbol schwa [ə] appears in several nonphonetic dictionaries, its use is not systematized. In some dictionaries it represents only the unstressed vowel of *sofa, effort,* or *awful,* etc. In at least one dictionary it has replaced the "short *ŭ*" (*bŭt*) in stressed syllables.

Some diacritics and respellings are intentionally ambiguous, representing several different but acceptable pronunciations. For example, some dictionaries provide a special diacritic for the *a* of *ask, last, half,* etc., since words in this group have several acceptable pronunciations in American English.

The dictionary most useful for settling arguments over differences in regional American pronunciations is the Kenyon and Knott phonetic dictionary mentioned earlier. However, many unabridged and college dictionaries give some information about regional differences in their introductory guides. There are also textbooks on the subject.

The rhythm of English words has much to do with both their stresses and the actual identity of their vowel sounds. Compare any group of related words on a page of your dictionary and notice how additional syllables and/or the shifting of stress may change the quality of a vowel. For example, compare *command, commander, commandery, commandment, commando,* but *commandant* and *commandeer; prefer, preferment,* but *preferable* and *preference; able, ably,* but *ability; sane, insane,* but *sanity, sanitation,* and *sanitarium.*

VARIATIONS IN PRONUNCIATION

No one with a clear understanding of the nature of language demands that all Americans use identical pronunciations. Modern dictionaries report variant pronunciations that the editors have found to be "actual educated speech" from all parts of the country, sometimes called "standard speech." Substandard pronunciations are variants occurring among uneducated speakers, who are at times in the majority. Therefore it is unwise to aspire to model your pronunciation merely after the majority, but rather the educated majority. Follow the habits of educated speakers, even if the pronunciation of the majority in some given locality may be different. Nor is it safe to defend your own pronunciation, when it is different from those recorded in your dictionary, by saying, "This is the way I

Fig. 7.4. Winston Churchill (*left*) and Edward R. Murrow (*right*) had distinctly different voices, yet both will always be remembered for their forceful and magnetic delivery.

always hear it." Very likely you have been exposed to an uneducated variation.

Suppose you and a friend have an argument about the pronunciation of a word. What are the possibilities?

1. You are both right. (There are two or more educated pronunciations used throughout the United States.)
2. You are both right. (You are using two different pronunciations used in *different parts* of the United States.)
3. One of you is right, the other wrong. (One is using a pronunciation avoided by the status group.)
4. You are both wrong. (Neither is using a commonly acceptable pronunciation.)

Such arguments over pronunciations grow out of the mistaken notion that every word has one and only one acceptable pronunciation, all others being inferior. No dictionary will support that idea. Any pronunciation appearing in a reputable dictionary without any label as to its low status is thought by the editors of that dictionary to be pronunciation spoken by a sufficient number of educated people to be acceptable to other educated people. "Substandard" pronunciations, i.e., pronunciations used by the uneducated, are excluded from dictionaries.

It should be admitted, however, that many educated people have strong preferences for some pronunciations and strong prejudices against others. In general, people are slow to approve and adopt changes in pronunciation, preferring the ones to which they have trained themselves. Therefore, if you wish to please the most discriminating of your listeners you might still do well to follow the old injunction:

> Be not the first by whom the new is tried,
> Nor yet the last to lay the old aside.

It is your responsibility to make your pronunciation not a liability but an asset to your speech.

QUESTIONS FOR INVESTIGATION AND DISCUSSION

1. Listen to some extremely informal conversation. Try to write approximately the sounds that were spoken rather than the conventional spelling. Your sample may look like this:

   "Jeet?" (Did you eat?)
   "No. Jew?" (No. Did you?)
   "Nah chet." (Not yet.)
   "Y on cha wadel weeken go together?" (Why don't you wait till we can go together?)

2. Listen to your local newscasters for both personal and regional peculiarities of pronunciation. Record the examples by respelling or by phonetic transcription. Do any of them interfere with communication?

3. Compare the diacritical marking systems of two dictionaries. For charts of similar comparisons consult Arthur J. Bronstein,

The Pronunciation of American English, Appleton-Century-Crofts, Inc., 1960, pp. 28–30, and Elise Hahn and others, *Basic Voice Training for Speech,* 2nd ed., McGraw-Hill Book Company, Inc., 1957, p. 132.

4. What are the causes of change in language? Consult Giles W. Gray and Claude M. Wise, *The Bases of Speech,* 3rd ed., Harper & Row, 1959, pp. 350–356, or other textbooks that discuss principles of language.

5. Why do people feel strongly about revisions of dictionaries? Read some articles attacking and defending the third edition of *Webster's New International Dictionary,* published in 1961. Use *Reader's Guide* to locate magazine articles on the subject.

6. Support or refute each of the following statements:

   The important thing is that we should speak, in a forceful, clear, and literate fashion, the variety of English of our upbringing.*

   If there is a margin of doubt, it is prudent to stay reasonably close to dictionary pronunciations, with due allowance for the variations which occur naturally in contextual speech.**

7. What are malapropisms? Analyze the text in which the originals occurred to determine what words were actually intended. Find contemporary examples in speeches and conversation to which you listen, and in your reading. What are the possible causes of these solecisms?

8. What spelling errors are you most likely to make? Are any of these possibly connected with errors in pronunciation? Are there grammatical errors seemingly associated with incorrect pronunciation?

9. What is "correct" pronunciation? Cite authorities to support your answer.

10. Visit your local broadcasting station and ask your newscaster about the sources of his information concerning new foreign names that he must pronounce in news reports.

11. Ask your librarian to recommend references that evaluate dictionaries for recommended purchase.

* Harold Whitehall in "The English Language," *Webster's New World Dictionary of the American Language,* College Edition, 1959, xvii.

** James A. Carrell and William R. Tiffany, *Phonetics: Theory and Application to Speech Improvement,* 1960, p. 9.

ASSIGNMENTS

In the exercises below, words are juxtaposed to call attention to both similarities and differences in spelling and pronunciation. Compare pronunciations. Be alert for surprises.

1. Distinguish between: *averse, adverse; core, corps, corpse, copse; Ur, "er," err, e'er, error, era; consul, council, counsel; tens, tents, tenets, tenants; abyss, abbess; long, longevity, chaise longue, lounge; oil, all; spacious, specious; credible, creditable; arrogate, abrogate; alleviate, alienate; similar, simulate.*

2. Note the possibility for mistaken analogy: *column, volume; corporate, cooperate; secret, secrete, secretive; grief, grievous, mischief, mischievous, heinous, barbarous, portent, portentous; length, width, breadth, height, weight; come, comely, home, homely; gem, gesture, orgy, gyroscope.*

3. Account for alternate pronunciations: *khaki, ration, route, robot, gala, rodeo, boatswain, leeward.*

4. Do you find unfamiliar or unexpected pronunciations for these? *Bade, victuals, breeches, creek, tarpaulin, comptroller, diphtheria, chagrin.*

5. Certain spelling letters and combinations of letters mislead the unwary:

oi: *coif, coiffure, du Bois, repertoire, repertory, connoisseur*
ui: *cuisine, ennui, suite*
l: *calm, alms, almond, salmon, palm, psalm, qualm, half*
gn: *sign, signal, malign, malignant, indignant, poignant*
el, le, ile: *muscle, vessel, missile, agile, docile, fragile, juvenile, infantile, senile, subtle*
en: *entree, envoy, ensemble*

6. Find the silent letters. Can you explain their presence? *Debris, debut, indict, arraign, writhe.*

7. Account for the varied pronunciations of the spelling *ch: charlatan, chateau, chattel, chauvinism, Cherokee, cheek, chic, Chekov, Chavez, choir, Chelsea, choreography.*

8. Ask your classmates and friends to express preferences for the pronunciations of these words: *toward, forehead, aria, theatre, drama, dramatist, piano, data, status, strata, alternate, alternative, Xavier.* Are all of their choices "standard" pronunciations?

9. Pronounce the following list of words *before* consulting your dictionary. Use analogy for those pronunciations of which you are unsure. Then check your responses against your dictionary. How reliable was analogy for you? *Ruthless, sagacious, salient, vagrant, unscathed, copious, demise, banal, deluge, disheveled, vagary, wont, slough, schism, bravado, scion, propitiate, cache, niche, acumen.*

SUGGESTED READINGS

Baugh, Albert C., *History of the English Language* (2nd ed.), Appleton-Century-Crofts, 1957.

Bronstein, Arthur J., *The Pronunciation of American English,* Appleton-Century-Crofts, 1960, chap. 1.

Carrell, James, and William R. Tiffany, *Phonetics: Theory and Application to Speech Improvement,* McGraw-Hill, 1960, chap. 1.

Evans, Bergen, "But What's a Dictionary For?" *The Atlantic Monthly,* **CCIX** (May, 1962), 57–62.

Fairbanks, Grant, *Voice and Articulation Drillbook* (2nd ed.), Harper & Row, chap. 9.

Follett, Wilson, "Sabotage in Springfield, Webster's Third Edition," *The Atlantic Monthly,* **CCIX** (January, 1962), 73–77.

Fries, Charles C., "Usage Levels and Dialect Distribution," *The American College Dictionary,* Harper & Row.

Gray, Giles Wilkeson, and Claude Merton Wise, *The Bases of Speech* (3rd ed.), Harper & Row, 1959, chap. 6.

Hahn, Elise *et al., Basic Voice Training for Speech* (2nd ed.), McGraw-Hill, 1957, chaps. 2 and 6.

Kantner, Claude E., and Robert West, *Phonetics* (rev. ed.), Harper & Row, 1960, chaps. 16 and 17. The latter chapter requires some understanding of phonetic transcription.

Kenyon, John S., *American Pronunciation* (10th ed.), Wahr, 1958. Requires considerable knowledge of phonetics.

Malmstrom, Jean, and Annabel Ashley, *Dialects—U.S.A.,* National Council of Teachers of English, 1963.

Sledd, James, and Wilma R. Ebbitt, *Dictionaries and THAT Dictionary,* Scott, Foresman, 1962. A casebook on lexicography with special attention to *Webster's Third.*

Whitehall, Harold, "The English Language," *Webster's New World Dictionary of the American Language,* College Edition, World Publishing, 1959.

Wise, Claude Merton, *Applied Phonetics,* Prentice-Hall, 1957, chap. 6.

░░░ VIII

HOW TO BE INTERESTING

The title of this chapter has been the object of a quest almost as popular as the search for a fountain of youth. Universally, persons strive for that indefinable quality that assures popularity. An adult speech course has built a significant part of its appeal on "how to win friends." Shelves of books have been written on how to develop charm and personality, how to acquire magnetism, poise, self assurance, optimism, tactfulness, perseverance, and initiative. But those who read widely on the subject and who struggle the hardest for mastery sometimes die of loneliness, while others who make almost no effort have hosts of friends.

Fig. 8.1. F.D.R. used dramatic gestures to create imagery, animation, and suspense.

In spite of the elusiveness of the subject, let us briefly try to pin down at least a few of the factors which make a speech interesting. Josh Lee, former public-speaking teacher, ex-senator from Oklahoma and a popular lecturer, summarizes interest factors in the following:

What does an audience want? Well, since the audience is made up of you and me, I'll ask again—what do *you* want? You want excitement, you want surprise, you want entertainment, you want the unusual. Ripley with his "believe it or not" is interesting because he deals with the unusual. You want suspense. You want the uncertain, or perhaps I should say, the undetermined. You want to be kept dangling before the answer is revealed. You want drama.

You want fun; you want humor—not cut and dried jokes which you could read in any joke book—but brilliant, scintillating wit fresh from a keen brain. You want that humor to be an integral part of the speech. You want imagery. You want word pictures which are similar to your own experiences and, therefore, stimulating. You want animation instead of "still life." You want action and conflict. You want concrete examples and not abstractions.[1]

FIND A NEW AND A DIFFERENT APPROACH

In any popularity contest based upon number of times delivered, Russell Conwell's "Acres of Diamonds," Wendell Phillips' "The Lost Arts," and William Jennings Bryan's "The Prince of Peace" would probably be far ahead of other American speeches. Chautauqua and lyceum audiences found these three speeches irresistible. Conwell delivered his speech over 6000 times from 1875 to 1925. Phillips gave his talk at least 2000 times over the period from 1838 through 1875; the Great Commoner thrilled audiences from 1900 until his death in 1925 with his favorite. Why were these talks so popular? To read them today provides no great inspiration. But at the time it was spoken each one ideally fitted the audience and the occasion; more important, the speakers developed their subjects in novel forms.

You will often do well with a familiar subject if you can find ways to clothe it in a bright new dress. For example, when he chose to speak on the old theme, "You should be sensitive to the needs of others," Kenneth I. Brown restated the proposition as: "Be men and women with antennae." To amplify this proposition, he rephrased it again, "No man is an island, neither can he live with an all-inclusive government of one." You can sense the flavor of how he developed his subject from a few paragraphs quoted below:

> No man is an island, neither can he live within an all-inclusive government of one. He needs that sensitiveness to the incipient emotions and heart-longings of others if he is to live as a responsible member of the human race. He needs a special competence in those media of communi-

[1] Josh Lee, *How To Hold An Audience Without A Rope*, Ziff Davis, 1947, pp. 85–86.

cation which are more difficult than the spoken language—the troubled eye, the quivering mouth, the withheld presence. Love is not alone the giving of self, even though that giving be generous and abundant. Love is the giving of self to another's need, and that need of the other can be learned not from generalizations about mankind nor from textbooks on psychology, but through the sensitive outreach of a human spirit touching gently another human spirit.

. . . The man without any antennae is the man who never quite comes into contact with his fellow human beings. He never sizes up the whole situation. He makes love into a self-thing because being without antennae he never touches the soul and the spirit of another.

There is something essentially tragic about the man who is unaware of the music in the air which he is not hearing, of the pictures in the air which he is not seeing. There is something essentially tragic about the man whose armor of personality prevents the subtle delicate shafts of human understanding that come from another, from penetrating into his own mind and heart.

One of the functions of education is to make us aware of the possibility of such understanding. Perhaps education is a process of building within us, according to the latest models, antennae which will allow us to move into direct contact with the spirit and the heart and the mind of another. I suppose that comes through the multiple and varied experiences of learning and living and loving. I am sure it comes in part through the human outreach that through understanding and compassion touches those around us.

Not only, however, do we need to be men and women with antennae. There is surging demand today that nations be nations with antennae, and with our concern for our beloved country, let us interpret this by saying, our United States needs especially to be a nation with antennae, catching the cries of the spirit, the suppressed longings of the other nations, large and small, in prosperity or in underprivilege.[2]

Through his supporting materials, Brown achieves novelty.

Of course, you may also achieve novelty through the way material is presented. Ralph Adams Brown dramatizes an idea by a clever play on organization. Notice how he used suspense in the last sentences:

I would like to discuss with you the "Three C's of Great Speaking." The first of these "C's" is *conviction*. . . .

[2] Kenneth I. Brown, "Men and Women With Antennae," *Vital Speeches of the Day*, **XXII** (August 15, 1956), 666–667.

Fig. 8.2. The resourceful speaker is constantly looking for different approaches and new angles.

Another component of a great speech is *courage*. . . .

I have enjoyed this opportunity to talk to you about *the three C's of great speaking.*

I have mentioned the three C's, have I not? Professors do get absent-minded, but I would not wish to omit part of my speech. You say I have only mentioned two?

Then I have not violated the third "C" of great speaking, for the third "C" is *conciseness.*[3]

[3] From speech by Ralph Adams Brown, "The Three 'C's' of Great Speaking," *Today's Speech,* **VII** (November, 1959), 16–17.

BE AS SPECIFIC AS POSSIBLE

The abstraction, the platitude, the overworked cliché, and the stereotype demand (and deserve) little attention or thought from the listener. When he hears an overworked phrase he is not challenged to reflect; consequently, he dismisses it without thought, or he goes to sleep, or he lets his thoughts drift to what is more important to him. Notice how Governor Mark O. Hatfield packed specific facts into three short sentences:

The 190,000,000 people of these United States share this terrestial ball with nearly 3 billion other human beings. There are, in other words, about 15 "foreigners" for every citizen of the United States of America. We are the fourth nation in terms of population but we stand first in most measures of material wealth.[4]

Ways to Be Specific

Below are listed ways to be specific:

1. Substitute concrete words for general words (See discussion of jargon, pp. 178–180).
2. Include exact names, dates, and places. Instead of referring to "a little Iowa town," say "Beacon, Iowa"; or instead of mentioning "a little place on a bayou," say "Napoleonville on Bayou Lafourche."
3. Include little details and side lights in your illustrations.
4. Strive to stir definite pictures (imagery) within the listener.
5. Speak in the first and second person.
6. Give personal experiences known only to yourself. At least you will know that your listeners will not have heard them before.
7. Mention incidents about listeners present or about persons well known to the listeners.
8. Refer to listeners by name or to authorities well known to listeners.

[4] Mark O. Hatfield, "Our Foreign Policy," *Vital Speeches of the Day*, **30** (June 15, 1964), 533.

Fig. 8.3. Walter Cronkite emphasizes a point with a specific example.

9. Insert asides, giving personal reactions or interpretations to material presented, especially quotations from others.
10. Present facts and ideas visually whenever possible.

Generally, the difference between effective and ineffective speaking is found in the factor of *concreteness*. The successful speaker gives personality to his speech through the way he elaborates, enlarges, and expands his ideas. He shows his skill through the manner he includes supporting materials to give life to what he says and

Th(NO3)4 soln.
+ NH3
ppt.
filtrate

"Continental Classroom," National Broadcasting Company

Fig. 8.4. Blackboard, movable chart boards and pointer enhance the speaker's message.

brings into play new interpretations. Whenever possible he sprinkles through his development "for example," "for instance," "to illustrate," and "to visualize." He may follow such a phrase with no more than a sentence or two while at other times he may give extended illustration, requiring several minutes to present.

Let us enumerate some kinds of examples:

1. Personal experiences
2. Incidents from lives of famous persons

3. Any historical examples
4. Hypothetical examples
5. The humorous stories
6. Allegories, fables, and parables
7. Analogies, figurative or literal
8. Case histories
9. Reports of experimentation
10. The reports on pilot projects

Notice how cleverly in the following illustration the speaker uses an analogy to make his point:

My next and last illustration comes also from Bold Island. I was looking out over the sea and then back to the tall pines rising a hundred feet above me and the thought came to me, "How fortunate I am to own this island." And then I reflected "You idiot! You do not, you cannot *own* this island. Some of those pine trees were looking across the channel one hundred years ago when the boys of the Maine regiment marched off to fight and die in the war between the states." Legally, I have the papers from the State of Massachusetts going back to the days when Maine was itself a possession of that older commonwealth. Legally, it is mine, spiritually I do not own it as much as it owns me.

And yet perhaps this is the answer, perhaps it is a kind of mutual ownership, for what I love I possess and am in turn possessed by it. Perhaps this is the answer to the eternal question of the art of music. We possess it and are in turn possessed by it. And in this joint possession we need to share our experience with others. We wish to become evangelists of the art. We wish to show the world that to the words the "search for truth" should be added that the equally important words the "search for beauty." For without beauty man must starve, without beauty man cannot live.[5]

Below are two versions of the same speech. Contrast the general treatment on the left with the more specific one on the right. Pay particular attention to the differences in concrete language and in the number of specific details.

[5] Howard Hanson, "The Place of Creative Arts: Failure to Fulfill Mission," *Vital Speeches of the Day*, **30** (November 15, 1963), 90.

The General Version	The Specific Version
Save the Big Trees	*Save the Redwoods*

The giant trees in northern California have been enjoyed by millions of people for many years. The chances are that people in the future are not going to be so lucky. The lumbering interests, well aware of the amount of board feet in each tree, have reduced the footage significantly between 1909 and 1953. The pace has continued at such a rapid rate that three quarters of the redwoods are gone. The end of these big trees will surely come soon if some steps are not taken.

If anyone wants to help save these forests, he can sent a ten-dollar contribution to the organization, Save-the-Redwoods League, in San Francisco.

Are you one of the fortunate Americans who has seen the magnificent coastal Redwoods in northern California? Your son and daughter may be denied this awe-inspiring experience. These graceful trees, alive two thousand years ago to greet the first Easter, are now over 20 feet in diameter and reach up as much as 350 feet. But even giants must struggle to survive. And they are losing. Persistent lumbermen are hacking away at them. In 1909, one hundred billion board feet of old growth stood against the high Pacific winds; by 1953 the amount had dropped to 35 billion board feet. Today three quarters of the Redwoods are gone forever.

Do you want to have a part in saving this oldest species of living things on earth? Send ten dollars to Save-the-Redwood, 114 Sansone Street, San Francisco, California.[6]

DRAMATIZE WHAT YOU SAY

The story technique remains a favorite way to gain and to hold interest. The good storyteller sweeps his listeners along as he sandwiches stories and illustrations in among his serious thoughts. Of course, one of the secrets back of Russell Conwell, who reportedly

[6] Adapted from Robert Rienow and Leona Rienow, "Goodbye to the Redwoods," *American Legion Magazine,* July, 1964, p. 47.

made five million dollars lecturing, was that he knew how to nail a point with a good story. His "Acres of Diamonds" is built around what happened to one Al Hafed, who lived not far from the River Indus. Greedy for diamonds, this discontented man sold his farm and wandered over the world in quest of riches. The next occupant of that same farm picked a great diamond from Al Hafed's garden brook. Conwell made his point—that opportunity is often near at hand where it is least expected. It should be emphasized that Conwell found his "acres of diamonds" in a technique of packing his talks full of stories and examples, many of which were taken from the lives of his eager listeners. Lecture-goers invited him back for a second and a third time to hear the same speech—or, almost the same; the stories were sometimes changed. The lesson of poor Al Hafed may inspire you to look close at hand for speech materials; Conwell's success will tell you to put them in a dramatic form.

Lawrence A. Dysart demonstrates how to dramatize a point. Notice how he drives home a point with a simple story:

Any message will be influenced by the experience of the person who sends it, especially so if he's a ten year old. When you receive a message, you interpret it in terms of your own experience. Isn't this true? I lived on an Arizona ranch most of my life before World War II. While in New Zealand, I met the girl who was later to become my wife. One day in Wellington, I called her up and invited her to have dinner with me. Dinner to me meant 12:00 noon—like it had always been on the ranch— breakfast, dinner, supper. Dinner to her meant candlelight and wine and it still does. I might have yet been standing in the lobby of the Midland Hotel, in Wellington, New Zealand, if, after cooling my heels for an hour, it had not, suddenly, dawned on me that our communication might have fallen down.[7]

There are many ways to dramatize elements of your speech. Professor Lionel Crocker of Denison College, a successful speech teacher and astute observer of speaking techniques, relates such an incident:

I shall never forget a returned missionary's illustration of the number of Christians there were in all India. He took from his pocket a tape many

[7] Lawrence A. Dysart, "Wanted: Effective Communicators," *Vital Speeches of the Day,* **29** (August 15, 1963), 669.

Fig. 8.5. Visual supports help the listeners to grasp and retain the point being developed.

yards long. On it he had indicated in different colors the various sects. He asked a member of the audience to run the tape to the back of the auditorium. Then with his fingers he pointed out the small section of the tape that represented how many Christians there were in comparison with other religions. Was that audience impressed![8]

If you have any doubt as to how the principle works, carefully observe several television commercials which, on many occasions, are more entertaining than the regular programs. Coca-Cola is reported to spend about $50,000,000 a year to dramatize the proposition, "Things go better with Coke." You hear it sung. You see it acted out. You see it advertized in newspapers and on billboards. It is posted on trucks, coolers, and buses. Even the Coke serviceman wears it on his uniform. Usually the advertiser does visually what you must accomplish mainly with words.

[8] Lionel Crocker, "Make the Illustration Linger," *Today's Speech,* **IV** (January, 1956), 4.

Presenting the Material

Below are some suggestions for selecting and presenting examples and narratives:

1. Select a story or illustration which clearly supports the point being developed.
2. Develop a significant punch or theme line at climax.
3. Carefully prepare introductory material to move quickly into development.
4. Eliminate details not absolutely essential to making point and holding interest. Err on the side of brevity.
5. Practice the presentation in order to perfect timing, pauses, and the surprise element. Good story telling appears to be unstudied, impromptu, spontaneous, and effortless.

KEEP THE LISTENERS GUESSING

The "whodunit" has an established place among novels, in the movies, and now on television because millions of Americans like to try to out guess the detectives and crime solvers. Perry Mason wins his case weekly before 25 million or more viewers. His creator Erle Stanley Gardner has written 73 Perry Mason novels which have sold over 100 million copies. Agatha Christie is not far behind in popularity. Here is a good lesson for the speaker: He who arouses curiosity and thereby keeps his listeners anticipating is likely to keep them listening actively to the end. You can use curiosity to tie a whole speech together or to amplify a single point. Below are some suggestions for creating and employing suspense:

1. Lead off with a provocative title such as "How Long Shall a Wife Live," "Merger of Spooks and Spitballs," "The Woman's Place Is In the Wrong," "He Walked Too Long Alone," "Are We Gaining or Guessing Abroad?"
2. Open with a startling question, statement, or announcement.
3. Employ the story technique, withholding the exciting incident or punch line until the end (see pp. 157–159).

4. Create doubt as to your real stand on an issue.
5. Insinuate that you plan to release a startling revelation during the speech.
6. Build your speech around a figurative statement or analogy.

However, it is *not* a good idea to give listeners a big build up which does not materialize. If, when you come to the climax, your listeners feel that you have tricked them or taken advantage of them, you are likely to lose their good will; they will not let you trap them a second time.

USE HUMOR TO CREATE AND HOLD INTEREST

Speakers have long realized the advantages of humor in speech-making. Some speakers believe that the funny story is the only way to open a speech. In fact, even Cicero, no mean orator, included a section on it in his *De Oratore,* published in 55 B.C. He has one of the characters in his dialogue say, "This talent . . . appears to me incapable of being communicated by teaching."[9] It certainly is true that some persons are much more successful with humor than others. Some have "it" and others don't. The indefinable "it" often defies analysis.

Purposes of Humor In a Speech

The essential aims for which humor can be utilized to reach are:

1. To recapture attention and interest.
2. To gain a favorable hearing.
3. To give emphasis to or to amplify a point.
4. To relieve tension or to disarm unsympathetic or hostile listeners.
5. To express good will toward listeners, showing appreciation for the listeners by deprecating yourself.
6. To serve as a thought break, that is, to permit the listeners to relax during or after a difficult presentation.
7. To cope with the unexpected or embarrassing incident.

[9] Cicero, *De Oratore* (Trans. J. S. Watson), Harper & Row, 1878, p. 144.

8. To answer a damaging attack of an opponent, turning the barb and recapturing the offensive.

Humor in a speech need not be confined to funny stories or jokes. James Winans observed that it may "spring from the turn of a phrase, from placing in juxtaposition an opponent's incongruous argument, from a comical bit of description, or narration, without going at all outside of the proper materials of the speech."[10] It varies greatly from person to person, and depends much on the circumstances. What produces healthy and prolonged laughter may indeed seem flat when told on another occasion, by a second person, or when put on the printed page. In considering Lincoln's "forte as a humorist and story teller," Roy P. Basler hints at this factor:

The stories for which he [Lincoln] was famed were generally confined to his impromptu speeches and personal conversation. . . . By all accounts they depended as much on grimace and mimicry as they did on inherent humor . . . hence many of them have become but poor reading as told second or third hand.[11]

Effective Use of Humor

Here are some guides to the effective use of humor:

1. Avoid humor if it is not your forte.
2. Use humor only when it forwards the purpose of the speech; if it does not support a point or have a definite purpose in the speaker's strategy, it should be omitted.
3. Make the humor grow out of the situation, turning the unexpected and the incongruous into an amusing story or clever turn of phrase.
4. Avoid "the old saws," the often repeated joke. Remember that other speakers may have read the same joke book and told the same joke before you arrived.
5. Keep your humor kind and congenial. Avoid dialect stories and caricatures involving religious and minority groups.
6. Keep humor in good taste, which means omitting profanity and obscenity.

[10] James Winans, *Speech-Making*, Appleton-Century-Crofts, 1938, p. 156.
[11] Roy P. Basler, *Abraham Lincoln: His Speeches and Writings*, World Publishing, 1946, pp. 15–16.

Fig. 8.6. It takes a wise speaker to know how—and when—to stop or to change his pace. This speaker clearly has lost his audience.

7. Get to the point quickly, keep humor brief.
8. Make the point of the humorous remark immediately apparent; humor depends upon its spontaneous quality.
9. Don't laugh at your own jokes—unless they are about yourself.

NOT TOO MUCH AT ONE TIME

How much is too much? Do you recall as a child developing a great eagerness for apples? You of course found the first one delicious; the second was not quite so tasty; but the third was no treat at all; and the fourth was unpleasant.

In planning your speech, don't forget your apple experience. It takes a wise speaker to know how to stop or to change his pace just before his listeners become weary and bored with him. Many preachers follow the 20-minute rule, saying that generally "no souls are saved after 12:00 noon on Sunday." Forgetting the apple principle, the college lecturer usually tries to struggle through 50 minutes, but when he persists in straight talking he has difficulty keeping his captive listeners with him throughout the entire period. Good listening requires a type of alertness which soon disappears when the material is complex, intricate in detail, or highly technical. You need to watch for signs of listening fatigue:

1. drowsiness
2. doodling
3. slumping back in chairs
4. lack of responsiveness
5. restlessness

QUESTIONS FOR INVESTIGATION AND DISCUSSION

1. What are the "factors of interest"? Check for these in another textbook; for example, see Giles W. Gray and Waldo W. Braden, *Public Speaking: Principles and Practice* (2nd ed.), Harper & Row, 1963, pp. 186–196.
2. How many of the factors of interest are implied in the suggestions given in this chapter?
3. How are attitudes, habits, and customs related to interest patterns?
4. Why are interests "strongest in old things in new settings"? Is the reverse true? How can the principle be employed in a speech?
5. Why do abstractions and stereotypes kill interest? How is it possible to kill interest by being too specific?
6. In what ways is choice of language associated with interest? How does figurative language contribute to interest?
7. What is "imagery"? How does it contribute to interest?
8. Under what circumstances might over-developed curiosity or anticipation detract from achieving the speech goal?
9. How do examples make a speech interesting? How are they related to the so-called "factors of interest"?

10. Under what circumstances would a reputation as a humorist serve as a handicap in effective speaking? See J. Jeffery Auer, "Tom Corwin: 'Men Will Remember Me as a Joker!' ", *Quarterly Journal of Speech*, **XXXIII** (February, 1947), 9–14.
11. Under what circumstances does the amusing story serve as a good opening for a speech? When is it not appropriate?
12. What are some fruitful sources of up-to-date humor? (Ask your librarian for help and prepare a list.)
13. What is meant by the so-called "attention span"? Why is this concept important to the speaker? Please find objective evidence on this concept.

ASSIGNMENTS

CLASS PROJECT

1. You are to prepare a five-minute informative talk on some aspect of the theme or problem which you selected in the previous assignment.

2. *For symposium groups:* You may wish to divide the material among the participants in such way that the class will receive a good overview of the entire theme.

3. If time permits, you will be asked to prepare a second informative talk on the topic.

SPEAKING ASSIGNMENTS

1. Deliver a five-minute speech in which you demonstrate one of the following principles:

a. Put an old theme in a new setting.
b. Make a specific application of an old principle.
c. Use an extended illustration or story to develop a serious thought.
d. Develop a speech inductively by first telling a series of stories and then drawing a conclusion.
e. Build suspense in a speech with proposition coming at the end.

2. Deliver five-minute speech on one of the following topics:

a. How humor saved the day.
b. How humor defeated a speaker.
c. How humor misfired.
d. The most amusing speaker I have ever heard.
e. An after dinner speech which succeeded (or failed).

RESEARCH ASSIGNMENTS

1. Deliver a five-minute analysis of the humor in a famous lecture. Consider carefully whether the speech is dated. What in the speech might account for its popularity? Examples of speeches you might consider:

"The Lost Arts" by Wendell Phillips
"Acres of Diamonds" by Russell Conwell
"The Sandwich Islands" by Mark Twain
"New England Weather" by Mark Twain

2. Analyze the speaking career of a speaker who won fame as a story-teller or an amusing speaker, considering a report on one of the following:

Auer, J. Jeffery, "Tom Corwin: 'Men Will Remember Me as a Joker!'", *Quarterly Journal of Speech*, **XXXIII** (February, 1947), 9–14.

Case, Victoria, and Robert Ormond Case, *We Called It Culture: The Story of Chautauqua*, Doubleday, 1948. See chapters on "Acres of Diamonds" and on William Jennings Bryan.

Clevenger, Theodore, Jr., "Alben W. Barkley's Use of Humor in Public Speaking," *Western Speech Journal*, **XX** (Winter, 1956), 15–22.

Reid, Loren D., " 'Private John' Allen: A Humorist in Politics," *Quarterly Journal of Speech*, **XXVIII** (December, 1942), 414–421.

BULLETIN BOARD ASSIGNMENT

Theme: Great Entertainers.

SUGGESTED READINGS

Bryant, Donald C., and Karl Wallace, *Fundamentals of Public Speaking* (3rd ed.), Appleton-Century-Crofts, 1960, chaps 7 and 16.

Gray, Giles Wilkeson, and Waldo W. Braden, *Public Speaking: Principles and Practice* (2nd ed.), Harper & Row, 1963, chaps. 11 and 26.

Grimes, Wilma H., "The Mirth Experience in Public Address," *Speech Monographs*, **XXII** (November, 1955), 243–255.

Gunderson, Robert G., "Lincoln's Rhetorical Style," *Vital Speeches of the Day*, **27** (February 15, 1961), 273–275.

Oliver, Robert T., Harold P. Zelko, and Paul D. Holtzman, *Communicative Speech* (3rd ed.), Holt, Rinehart and Winston, chap. 8.

IX

HOW TO BE CLEAR

Probably the most common type of speech is the informative. Parents, foremen, scoutmasters, guides, teachers must be expert in this type of speaking, for their success depends upon how effectively they can move their listeners toward understanding, mastery, and retention of the information they are presenting.

Imparting understanding or encouraging the development of insight involves presenting new facts or relationships, sharpening the powers of observation and discrimination, correcting misinformation, breaking old habits, developing new skills and techniques.

Moving one step further, the gaining of mastery involves conditioning, drill, and performance under supervision. The final step is making the skill acquired habitual, or fastening the new information in the memory. There seems to be little point to developing understanding unless the listener will retain what you have said over a considerable length of time.

TYPES OF INFORMATIVE TALKS

The Simple Explanation

The most common type of informative talk involves giving instructions or directions to a listener. At the simplest level, you may give directions to the listener, perhaps answering a simple request for information. The teacher making a class assignment or the foreman explaining a new tool are examples of this type of speech.

The How-To-Do-It Speech

In the how-to-do-it speech, the speaker teaches the listener how to perform a simple skill or to operate an apparatus, such as how to grip a tennis racket, how to bake a cake, how to stop a faucet drip, or how to select a new hammer.

Informative Description

An important type or aspect of information-giving involves creating a word picture or the enumeration of details and relating a whole and its parts. It also involves showing how a case or instance or thing is different from other members of its class. It is associated with the presentation of new models, a layout, or a display. For example, an architect describes for a client a new home, or a teacher tells his students about the Roman Forum. It may also include the portrayal of qualities and attitudes as well as material objects.

Informative Narrative

The informative narrative is concerned with the accurate reporting of a sequence of events. It may present the steps of a process or a procedure. Other common types are (1) autobiography, (2) biographical sketch, (3) travelogue, and (4) the historical account.

Fig. 9.1. Simple explanations frequently occur in all types of speaking situations. They become most important in the informal seminar.

The informative narrative seeks to give information but to avoid emotional coloring and loaded words. It should not be confused with storytelling that entertains.

KNOW YOUR SUBJECT THOROUGHLY

Successful information-giving starts with having a clear picture of what you wish to present. You must have command of considerably more details than you can present within the time allotted to your presentation. You will discover that systematic and careful preparation provides the same kind of confidence and assurance that comes from having money in the bank. A savings account offers

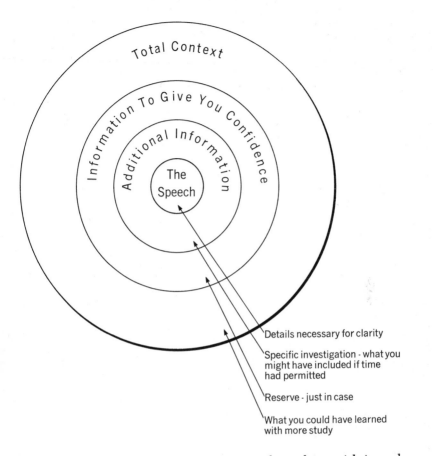

Fig. 9.2. Systematic and careful preparation of speech materials is much like the systematic and careful budgetary attention required for building a savings account—and leads to a similar result. The material is there when you need it and assures you confidence.

that little cushion against disaster. The fact that you have funds available for emergency brings inner calm and assurance important for happy living. Similarly, you will discover that careful analysis and study before delivery will serve you well when you face your listeners and when you meet the unexpected or with demands for amplification and additional examples. You will not be embarrassed by extending yourself to the very edge of your information.

Large businesses and industries caught up in complicated procedures and multiple operations prepare brief manuals or printed instructions in order to facilitate training. These materials have the advantages of saving the instructional time. Close at hand, the teacher has all the immediate details he needs for his talk. But what is the disadvantage? He may discover that he has difficulty making these terse materials his own; consequently, he suffers from a lack of self-assurance. He gains much by moving through a process or procedure step by step, by attempting to anticipate questions, by looking for new insights, and by striving to find ways to simplify his presentation. He discovers that the more he learns about a subject the more he profits from the money-in-the-bank principle.

Unfortunately, many persons who must rely on prepared materials or who are satisfied with a digest for information are not made aware of the money-in-the-bank principle until they encounter a bright questioner who has insatiable curiosity and who insists on asking questions not covered in the digest or manual. A bright listener will soon convince almost any speaker that it is wise to know as much as possible about a subject.

Let us repeat! A first important step in being *clear* is to know your subject, to have a sharp picture of what you wish to present, to be expert in manipulating the materials or tools involved. Understanding comes through objectivity, accuracy, and thoroughness.

KNOW YOUR LISTENERS THOROUGHLY

High-school and college students are well aware of what happens when a teacher makes no attempt to study his listeners. Every campus has its Professor Snarf who always aims too low or too high. This type either in an overly solicitous mood "insults their intelligence" by talking down to his students, or he absent-mindedly "talks over their heads," never considering their capacity for understanding. The first method produces disgust and rebellion and destroys the speaker's ethos; the second creates disinterest, boredom, and often sleep.

Analyzing listeners for an informative talk involves a consideration of the following listener characteristics.

1. Intellectual ability
2. Previous information, training, and experience
3. Understanding of the vocabulary necessary for the presentation
4. Interest and involvement in the subject
5. Ability and opportunities to see and hear the presentation
6. Familiarity with the type of presentation whether it is a lecture, discussion, demonstration, or film showing
7. Training and ability in note-taking, listening, and retaining the information
8. Handicaps resulting from previous conditioning and learning
9. Psychological blocks against learning, mastery, and retention

Some Important Questions To Be Asked

In analyzing your listeners, you should also raise the following questions:

1. In what ways are the listeners homogeneous in their abilities: listening, learning, and retention?
   a. Years of school?
   b. Mental age?
   c. Special or technical training?
   d. Practical experience?
2. What do the listeners know about the specific subject to be presented?
   a. What are their sources of information?
      (1) Self-trained and educated?
      (2) Formal schooling?
      (3) Training programs, short courses?
      (4) Practical experience?
      (5) Hearsay and casual encounter?
   b. How well are they informed ?
      (1) Uninformed?
      (2) Casual acquaintance?
      (3) Average information?
      (4) Skilled or above average?
      (5) Expert or professional?
   c. Does the subject involve any taboos or threats to the listeners?
      (1) Religious?

   (2) Social?

   (3) Community?

   (4) Occupational?

  3. Are the listeners captives?

   a. Are they paid to attend?

   b. Are there social pressures to attend?

   c. What hazards are involved for not participating?

   d. What are the rewards and punishments for learning?

  4. What motives promise greatest success for involvement?

   a. Pride?

   b. Praise?

   c. Fear?

   d. Ridicule?

   e. Some other motive?

  5. What are the levels of aspiration?

WORK FOR SIMPLE AND CLEAR ORGANIZATION

The suggestions made in Chapter III concerning oral organization certainly are most important for an informative speech. Particularly important are the following:

1. Keep your organization before the listeners at all times, using a preview, short points, restatement, and summaries. When possible write your main points on the chalk board or still better, display them on flow chart or strip chart (see Fig. 9.3). At frequent intervals indicate the point under discussion at the moment.

2. Arrange your presentation by one principle only, staying throughout the speech with an arrangement such as:

   Time order (flow or developmental)

   Space order

   Topical order

   Functional order

3. Word your central thought and each main point in short simple declarative sentences.

4. Avoid more than five points. When you have more than five you need to revise, consolidate, and simplify.

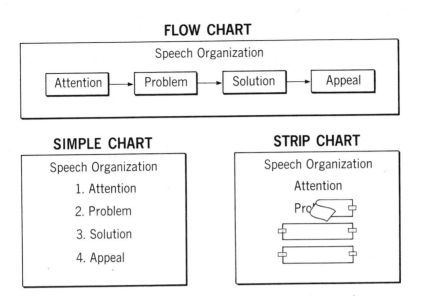

Fig. 9.3. Charts are valuable in keeping points before the listeners.

AS MANY LISTENER CUES AS POSSIBLE

A listener cue is any device or signal which helps the auditor to spot points and to follow the order and progress of the speech. Since listening is a difficult and inexact process, and since your listeners may encounter distractions, you should include devices which suggest the progression of ideas and what is important.

Let us list a few of the types of listener cues available to you:

1. Enumerating and labeling main points. Notice in the following examples the words in italics:

> *Three major problems* stand in the way of a better world for all people. *The first* is that of diminishing resources. . . .
> *The second major cloud* obscuring the hope for civilization is. . . .
> *The third and at present the most crucial problem* clouding the future for mankind. . . .[1]

2. Phrases which make clear the speaker's position: "I have had much experience. . . ."; "I consider these procedures unsound";

[1] Frances H. Horn, "The Prospect of Civilization," in Lester Thonssen (Ed.), *Representative American Speeches: 1962–1963*, H. W. Wilson, 1963, pp. 82–96.

"I believe that this procedure is well developed"; "In my opinion. . . ."; "My hunch is. . . ."

3. Phrases which show what is important: "The most important point is. . . ."; "Now get this point"; "This operation is vital"; "Don't miss this point"; "Let me stress what is important."

4. Phrases which make clear time or space relationships: "On the right side"; "Next to the roof"; "Just below the window"; "Fifteen hundred years ago. . . ."; "A week ago I discovered. . . ."

5. Statements which suggest development or where the speaker is in the speech: "In the introduction I shall. . . ."; "Summing it up. . . ."; "Now that we have considered the first two points. . . ."; "I shall conclude in two minutes."

MAKE USE OF MULTISENSORY CHANNELS

The senses are the channels through which you must reach your listeners. As a rule, making use of two more channels will increase your effectiveness. In other words, the speaker who presents his message visually as well as orally is likely to stimulate greater attention and interest and gain greater retention than the speaker who sticks entirely to the lecture method. Of course, the speaker who demonstrates how to prepare some delicious dish may also bring the olfactory as well as gustatory senses into play.

The rule is simple: Strive to utilize as many channels as possible.

Visual supports such as chalkboard sketches, charts, maps, flannel boards, models, specimens, film strips, and motion pictures involve multisensory appeals. Let us enumerate some of the ways to increase the effectiveness of the visual supports (Fig. 9.4):

1. Make drawings large enough so that all listeners can see with ease.
2. Write, print, or draw clearly and legibly.
3. Keep labels short and simple.
4. Avoid including unnecessary details in your drawing.
5. Arrange visuals in steps, moving in a prearranged direction.
6. Employ schematic drawings, emphasizing important features.
7. Don't crowd material in layout, distributing it well over chart

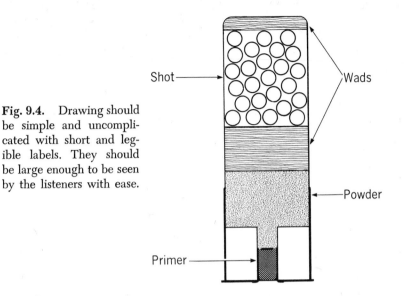

Shot — Wads

Powder

Primer

Fig. 9.4. Drawing should be simple and uncomplicated with short and legible labels. They should be large enough to be seen by the listeners with ease.

8. Avoid including material which does not support point under consideration.
9. Include colors only when they will add dimension to the meaning.
10. Draw or write quickly to prevent a lag of interest.
11. Place the visual support where every person can see it with ease.
12. Fit visual support into development at moment it supports point. If possible, keep visuals concealed until you use them in your presentation. Don't let them steal attention.
13. Employ a pointer when possible to focus attention and to avoid obstructing view.
14. When giving a demonstration, give listeners opportunities to see the object from many different positions and not just from one side or from one angle.

SUPPLEMENT ORAL PRESENTATION WITH DEMONSTRATION

The most exciting period in many lower lementary grades is the "show and tell" period. A first grade teacher is never surprised at what her 6-year-olds bring to class; she knows that "showing" with "telling" makes for exciting communication. Any communicator can learn something from these little people. Keep *telling* and *showing* as a part of the same presentation.

The straight lecture too often goes straight from the speaker's notes to the student's notebook with little thought in between. It is often in one direction with little feedback to indicate whether the speaker is getting through. As a rule, keep *telling* to a minimum in order to give more time to *showing* and supervised performance. Successful communication moves though a four-step process:

Explanation → Demonstration → Performance by learner →
Critique by teacher

Here are a few suggestions to improve your demonstration:

1. Fit the demonstration into the presentation without delays and without disrupting the speaking situation.
2. Focus the demonstration on specific points covered in presentation.
3. Keep your demonstration short.
4. Tie the demonstration and its application together.
5. Perform the demonstration with ease; when the instructor is awkward, the learner questions his own ability to perform the project.

AVOID JARGON AND ABSTRACT LANGUAGE

Few speakers like to admit that they ever use *jargon,* for the word carries an unpleasant and discomforting connotation. Simply defined, *jargon* is a collective term for a specialized and often idiomatic vocabulary used by a group of persons who work together or who engage in similar activities. Lawrence A. Dysart of the Richfield Oil Company nicely characterizes jargon—or "gobbledygook" as he calls it—as "a monster with many heads. It never uses one word if it can use two or more. Gobbledygook builds big words out of little ones. It loses sight of the fact that the more simply arranged a sentence is, the easier it is to understand."[2]

---

[2] Lawrence A. Dysart, "Wanted: Effective Communicators," *Vital Speeches of the Day,* **29** (August 15, 1963), 669.

Fig. 9.5. Demonstrations with actual machines are particularly important in topics as complicated as radar.

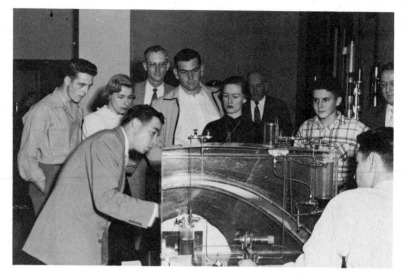

Fig. 9.6. Difficult, technical, or highly specialized presentations should be kept as free of jargon and abstract language as possible.

As long as you speak to close associates, you encounter no problems with such language. *Technical language* likewise becomes *jargon* when you move outside your little circle. When the linemen of the telephone company speak of "pole-burners," they understand that they are referring to themselves, but the phrase is meaningless to others. Teenagers understand what they mean by the term "cool," but adults are completely mystified by it.

What does the following sentence mean to you? "In this *materialistic* age, when the forces of *so-called* modernisation ensure the teenager is bombarded with sex, it is hardly surprising that the standards of a *more leisured age* are vanishing."[3] Suppose someone says to you, "Let's up-periscope and look around." Would you know what he meant? If you are in a certain advertising firm, you would realize that he had invited you to predict the future.

Or consider the following paragraph reported to have been the conclusion of a speech:

[3] Katharine Whitehorn, in the London *Observer,* November 3, 1963.

The time has come to put the compass on the table and see which way is north. Fight! Hit that line and hit it hard! I'll just talk off the top of my head but I know you'll get the picture. We're all a team, a big team, we're all fighting for the same thing—better shows. You say, no business like show business but, men, if we want to stay alive, we've got to make more money. Cut costs, cut them intelligently. That great leader of us all, our big coach in Washington, is showing us the way. We're little men, but we can do our part, too. And now, I'm gonna pass the ball to our quarterback.[4]

To restate the principle: Clarity results from putting your thoughts into the language of your listeners. We can agree with Aristotle that "good style is, first of all, clear."

MAKE YOUR STATISTICS MEANINGFUL

Statistics constitute a specialized way of presenting facts. When well used, they give substance to a speech, but when not they confuse and discourage understanding. The engineer or scientist, eager to be accurate, may include several complex tables, difficult graphs, long lists, complex computations. As a result he soon loses his listeners—even those who are accustomed to following a statistical development.

Put yourself in the shoes of your listener; then attempt to put your statistics in form for listening—not for reading and study. Here are five suggestions to help you reach your listeners:

1. Round off your statistics. Instead of giving the number down to the last digit, give perhaps an approximate one, such as nine and a quarter million.
2. Present your statistics in a familiar form. With Americans, miles, yards, feet, and inches are more acceptable than kilometers, meters, and centimeters. Pints, quarts, pecks are more familiar than liters. When in Rome do as the Romans.
3. Translate your statistics into visual form whenever possible. For example, a bar or line graph will make statistical relationships

---

[4] Quoted in John Crosby, "Madison Avenue Mother Tongue," *Lansing* (Michigan) *State Journal*, July 20, 1953.

YOUR SPEECH GRADES

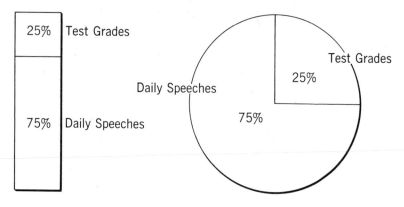

Fig. 9.7. Translate your statistics into visual form wherever possible.

clearer. You must take care however to orient the listeners as to the step intervals of the abscissa and those of the ordinate:

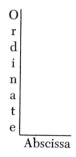

4. Put your statistics in dramatic form. To make your facts stick longer with the listeners, search for striking comparisons and novel ways to present them. Below are two excellent examples of this method:

While the ordinary light microscope enlarges a specimen to about 2000 times life size, the electron microscope can blow it up more than 300,000 times. At this degree of magnification, an ant would become a colossus able to stand astride the St. Lawrence River.[5]

[5] John L. Burns, "The Endless Frontier," *Vital Speeches of the Day,* **27** (October 15, 1960), 21–24.

Consider the age of the majestic Redwoods in California, the world's tallest trees. Some are 3000 years old. Imagine their beginnings before old Homer first told his stories in ancient Greece. They were a thousand years old when Christ walked in Galilee.

DEFINE UNFAMILIAR TERMS

Remember that words carry the load of a message. You can stir up little meaning when your listener fails to understand key terms and phrases. You find convincing proof of this statement when, in translating a foreign language, one or two unfamiliar words completely thwart you. To announce that you intend to discuss the operation of a lorry may produce real puzzlement until you add that lorry is the British word for motor truck. If you speak of spending a holiday in a caravan, Americans might conclude that you had been on a desert mission over the Fourth-of-July. To an Englishmen, it means perhaps a week at the seaside living in a trailer. In Louisiana, many persons use the phrase, "this evening," to mean sometime after 2:00 P.M. but in Iowa, it means after 6:00 P.M. If words are to link speaker and listener, they must suggest essentially the same to both.

What types of words or phrases cause the least difficulty? Name words referring to concrete objects are least likely to confuse. When you and your listeners can see, touch, smell, or taste what you are discussing, you are likely to find common agreement. For example, to let the listeners *see* a toggle bolt, a C-clamp, or a corrugated fastener improves your chances of successful communication. Still better is to give each listener a sample to examine with his own hands. If you are speaking about the apteryx—a New Zealand bird—a drawing, photograph, or motion picture may indeed save you a thousand words.

The type of words that are most likely to cause misinterpretations are those referring to concepts, qualities, and attitudes. Notice that these are words encompassing other words. Figurative language is also open to a variety of interpretations. Such words are high-level abstractions, implying that they move away from concreteness. For example:

Concepts: democracy, communism, standard of living, charity, poor white, wordmonger.

Qualities: good, bad, effectiveness, pleasant, beautiful, enjoyable.

Figurative language: "Life is just a bowl of cherries," "cool car," "hot rod," "cheesecake," "leg show," "brush-fire wars," "flag waving."

When you sense that a word may result in misinterpretation or confusion, you need to consider one of the following methods of definition:

1. Give a dictionary or accepted definition:

Jettison refers to casting all or part of a ship's cargo overboard to lighten the vessel or to meet some danger such as a fire.

Applied phonetics is the study of significant speech sounds.

2. Give the class of the word and differentiate it from other members of the class:

A tandem is a bicycle with two seats placed one behind another.

3. Give several synonyms:

An enthusiast may be a zealot, a fanatic, or a devotee.

Nonconformity is referred to as heterodoxy, disaffection, secession, or recantation.

4. Explain what the word does *not* mean (definition by negation):

Applied phonetics does not include the study of grammar.

Rhetoric does not refer to the excessive or extravagant use of words; in this context it implies the theory of persuasive speaking.

5. Trace the etymology or derivation of a word, showing how the meaning has developed:

Lagniappe is a Louisiana-French version of the American-Spanish *la napa*, meaning "the gift." It is properly applied to something given with a purchase to a customer over and beyond what was bargained for.[6]

Cajun is a corruption of the word *Acadian*, referring to native Louisianians of French ancestry.

[6] Bergen Evans, *Comfortable Words*, Random House, 1962, p. 224.

Underground originally referred to an underground railroad which before the Civil War was a scheme to help slaves escape from the South to Canada. During World War II its meaning changed to imply a secret organization fighting the German occupational forces.

6. Compare the word or concept with a word or concept familiar to the listeners:

An aardvark is like an anteater.

7. Use a word in context. A word never stands alone; it gives of itself to its neighbors, and they are influenced by its meaning. Furthermore, a word never means the same—maybe almost the same, but not exactly the same—to two different persons or in two different usages. Therefore, to explain the meaning of word in isolation is often misleading and confusing. You help your listener to understand by including words in context and then interpreting the implications. Observe how Justice William O. Douglas suggests what free speech means to him:

My thesis is that there is no free speech in the full meaning of the term unless there is freedom to challenge the very postulates on which the existing regime rests. It is my belief that our First Amendment must be placed in that broad frame of reference and construed to permit even discourse or advocacy that strikes at the very foundation of our institutions. The First Amendment was a new and bold experiment. It staked everything on unlimited public discussion. It choose conflicting values, selecting the freedom to talk, to argue, and to advocate as a preferred right. It placed us on the side of free discussion and advocacy, come what may.[7]

CHECKING YOUR FEEDBACK

"Do they understand what I am saying?" is a question which should continually nag you when you are giving an informative talk. To satisfy this type of anxiety, you need actual feedback; that is, listener reactions to what you are saying. What type of reactions will give you hints concerning your effectiveness? Below are some typical signs:

[7] William O. Douglas, *The Right of the People*, Pyramid Books, 1962, pp. 9–10.

Fig. 9.8. In demonstrations, feedback should be encouraged and promoted.

1. Facial expressions showing either interest or disinterest, approval or disapproval (Fig. 9.8)
2. Shifts in body positions indicating receptivity or restlessness
3. Movement such as changing seats or leaving the room
4. Overt expressions of approval or disapproval: laughter, boos, amens, from-the-floor comments
5. Willingness to follow speaker's suggestions: quieting down, opening a window, moving closer, assisting with presentation
6. Questions from the floor

Of course, these signs are indeed fallible as an experienced speaker is well aware. Listeners may fake attentiveness in order to please you or the controlling authority, to avoid less pleasant activities, or to escape censure or punishment. Most college professors know how skillful students are in appearing to listen when they are miles away in their daydreams, or how willing they are to laugh at stale and trite jokes. In business and industry, the "yes"-man thrives because employees have discovered that preferment comes with agreeing with the boss. Many ministers are skeptical of the feedback they get from their listeners, who often put on expressions of mock reverence.

William R. Simmons, Ford Foundation

Fig. 9.9. Listener questions can enliven—or fatally disrupt—a discussion. As a speaker, you must control the direction you want them to take.

As a speaker, you must sort out the meaningful, honest feedback from the sham or misleading responses. Because you are human, you are likely to be receptive to, and eager for, favorable response. But you must not become susceptible to flattery. *One of the best types of feedback is through the direct questions you can elicit.*

Ways To Stimulate Questions

Questions from the listener truly make communication a two-way process, but as the speaker you need to get the ball rolling. Below are 15 suggestions:

1. Discuss a subject in which the listeners are intensely interested.
2. Develop a rapport and establish common ground with listeners.
3. Demonstrate an eagerness to have questions from listeners.

4. Answer questions fairly and honestly.
5. Treat the questioner with courtesy and fairness—even when his questions are irrelevant.
6. Express your appreciation for a good question by complimenting the questioner.
7. Plant questions with selected listeners to get interchange started.
8. Alert a selected listener to be prepared to ask a question.
9. Use a buzz-group technique, letting three or four listeners join together to frame questions.
10. Permit members to write out questions—in order to permit them to remain anonymous.
11. Offer to answer embarrassing questions in private conference.
12. Solicit questions from persons with whom you are well acquainted, or who have particular points of view.
13. Phrase and answer an overhead or typical question.
14. Help a listener to phrase his question.
15. Dare the listener to ask a question (a questionable technique).

Ways To Discourage Questions

Now let us look at the other side of the coin and note some ways by which speakers discourage or choke off questions. *These methods are to be avoided:*

1. Speak at an excessive rate, making it difficult to cut in.
2. "Pull rank," dismissing a question of subordinate.
3. Lecture the listeners on what they should and should not know and about what they should ask questions.
4. Read from manuscript and never look at listeners, appearing confused when you are interrupted.
5. Emphasize that you cannot possibly finish your speech in the time available.
6. Schedule questions immediately before a break, a lunch hour, or toward the end of a period.
7. Ridicule or make fun of irrelevant questions.
8. Insist that the questioner stand and identify himself.
9. Give evasive answers to questions.
10. Refuse to answer questions.

11. Anticipate what the question is before the questioner has a chance to ask it.
12. Delay answering until it is more convenient for you.

What Questions Tell You About Your Listeners

If the speaker has developed an atmosphere of mutual respect and one conducive to questioning, he should be able to get the following direct insights from the questions his listeners ask:

1. Whether the listener understood and remembers what has been said
2. What gaps exist in the understanding of the listeners
3. Whether resistance or opposition have developed from what has been presented
4. Whether the listeners have related what has been presented to the problem at hand
5. Whether further information is needed for the listener to utilize fully what has been presented

Thus, a question not only seeks information, it reveals how well the listener understands the presentation and how he feels about the speaker and his manner of presentation. To illustrate what you can learn indirectly through listener questions, let us consider four question situations:

1. Suppose the listener asks searching question about the subject matter under consideration. The possibilities with reference to listener are:
   a. Inability to hear
   b. Not afraid of the speaker
   c. Unfamiliar with terminology
   d. Interest in subject
   e. Conscientious and eager to succeed
   f. Eagerness to attract your attention
2. Suppose the listener asks questions about material which you believe has already been covered sufficiently. The possibilities are:
   a. You have not covered material adequately
   b. The questioner is lagging behind others

    c. Questioner has not paid close attention

    d. Questioner is probably missing what is being presented at the moment

3. Suppose the listener asks a question about unrelated material; the possibilities are:

    a. You have not made your subject and its limits clear

    b. The listener is completely confused about the subject

    c. The listener is attempting to lead you off the subject for some reason, such as avoiding recitation

    d. The listener is attempting to show off

4. Suppose the listener demonstrates antagonism by his question (in the army, this type was called a sharpshooter). The possibilities are:

    a. You have been discussing a subject about which listener is sensitive

    b. The listener is a captive who resents being required to listen to you

    c. The listener dislikes you, your subject, or the way you are presenting it

    d. The listener wants to show off

QUESTIONS FOR INVESTIGATION AND DISCUSSION

1. How is a descriptive speech to inform different from a literary description?

2. How is an informative narrative different from an entertaining narrative?

3. As a rule, how much can you expect your listeners to remember from an informative talk?

4. Under what circumstances are visual aids most useful in an informative speech?

5. In what ways may visual aids be used in a speech? Find examples of each.

6. What types of visual aids are available to you in presenting your classroom speeches?

7. What types of visual supports does the speaker have within himself?

8. What are some original ways of making statistics meaningful? (Look for methods not presented in chapter.)

9. What do the following terms and phrases mean: "Words are only symbols," "levels of abstraction," "high-level abstractions," "careless use of 'is'," "indiscriminate use of 'all'," "careless use of 'either . . . or' relationships." Consult a book on general semantics, such as S. I. Hayakawa, *Language in Thought and Action* (2d ed.), Harcourt, Brace & World, 1964.

10. How can you deal with the questioner who seeks to disrupt your presentation?

11. What are several ways to stir the listeners to ask questions?

12. What insights into personality can you gain by observing how a speaker handles questions?

ASSIGNMENTS

CLASS PROJECT

1. *Problem phase:* Each member of the class is to prepare a five-minute speech on the problem phase of theme or problem.

2. *Solution phase:* Each member is to prepare a five-minute speech on the solution to the problem.

3. *Informal debate:* Divide into pairs, pro and con—or divide into equal teams. Each pair will present a short informal debate. After a speaker gives his main speech of 5 minutes, he will submit to 3 minutes of questioning by his opponent.

4. *Appeal speech:* Each member will deliver a stirring, four-minute appeal for action on his proposal.

SPEAKING ASSIGNMENTS

1. Deliver a five-minute informative talk in which you tell the class how to construct a map locating your home. Ask members of the class to draw the map as you give instructions. When you have finished your speech, collect the maps, and see how effective you

were in giving simple instructions. Write a brief estimate of your effectiveness.

2. Deliver a five-minute informative talk in which you use one of the following types:

    a. An informative description of a building in your home town
    b. An informative narrative of a trip you have taken
    c. A historical narrative

3. Deliver a five-minute explanation of a plan of organization, a procedure, or an operation.

4. Deliver a five-minute talk in which you attempt to make the audience appreciate a great distance, a great value, or a great size.

5. Deliver a five-minute visual aids speech. Use a chart or flannel board in the presentation.

6. Deliver a five-minute talk on one of the following topics:

    a. How an instructor makes his presentation clear through the use of visual aids
    b. An instructor with an unusual teaching method
    c. How a speaker dramatized his statistics
    d. How an instructor dramatizes his subject matter

RESEARCH ASSIGNMENTS

1. Collect several examples of jargon. You may find these in textbooks, in magazines, in the newspaper, or in speeches.

2. Collect several examples of how a speaker put his statistics in a dramatic form. Consult *Vital Speeches of the Day.*

3. Collect several examples of how speakers made an unfamiliar term or phrase clear.

BULLETIN BOARD ASSIGNMENT

Theme: Speakers Using Visual Aids.

SUGGESTED READINGS

Braden, Waldo W., and Earnest Brandenburg, *Oral Decision-Making,* Harper & Row, 1955, chap. 7.

Brigance, William Norwood, *Speech: Its Techniques and Disciplines in a Free Society* (2nd ed.), Appleton-Century-Crofts, 1961, chap. 11.

Bryant, Donald C., and Karl R. Wallace, *Fundamentals of Public Speaking* (3rd ed.), Appleton-Century-Crofts, 1960, chap. 9.

Gray, Giles Wilkeson, and Waldo W. Braden, *Public Speaking, Principles and Practice* (2nd ed.), Harper & Row, 1963, chaps. 18 and 25.

Lomas, Charles W., and Ralph Richardson, *Speech: Idea and Delivery* (2nd ed.), Houghton Mifflin, 1963, chap. 5.

Loney, Glenn M., *Briefing and Conference Techniques*, McGraw-Hill, 1959.

Monroe, Alan H., *Principles and Types of Speech* (5th ed.), Scott Foresman, 1962, chaps. 16 and 17. This book is recognized for its presentation of the five-step motivated sequence involving attention, need, satisfaction, visualization and action.

X

HOW TO BE PERSUASIVE

Persuasion plays an important part in all of our activities. We use it in our daily lives, in our professional associations, at church and of course in the public forum. During presidential elections we have many demonstrations of persuasion at work. For example at the 1964 Republican National Convention, Nelson Rockefeller, Mark Hatfield, and Barry Goldwater exercised to the utmost the art of persuasive speaking.

A persuasive speaker consciously attempts to achieve with his listeners one or more of the following objectives.

Fig. 10.1. Nelson Rockefeller—like other politicians—strives to gain acceptance and action.

1. To stir up attitudes favorable to his cause
2. To gain acceptance of his opinions or beliefs
3. To move to action

On a given occasion, the speaker may strive to accomplish only one of these objectives, or he may incorporate two or three in the same speech. How far he moves his listeners depends on how firmly his listeners hold to their old positions.

The persuasive speaker seeks to change his listeners because he finds them in one of the following unsatisfactory conditions:

1. Unaware or uninterested in problem
2. Unwilling, hesitant, or not enthusiastic to join in solving problem

3. Baffled about how to solve problem
4. Unable to agree upon a single solution
5. Tired or weary of working on the solution
6. Unaware of significance of their efforts

THREE KINDS OF PERSUASIVE GOALS

The Stimulating Goal

This goal is best characterized by the sentence: *Please be enthusiastic.* Having this goal, the speaker attempts to stir up or to strengthen latent but favorable attitudes or feelings. He seeks to rekindle and to heighten appreciation (admiration or veneration) for a man, an institution, an ideal, a virtue, an issue, or an event. This type of goal results in pep talks, good-will speeches, commendations, commemorations, eulogies, commencement addresses, and some sermons. Some typical propositions for this type of speech are:

1. John F. Kennedy was a great American.
2. State University must win tomorrow.
3. No man is an island.
4. Conservatism is the only hope for the United States.
5. We cannot solve your problems through violence.
6. Love thy neighbors.
7. Let's make Baton Rouge the football capital of the United States.

The Convincing Goal

This goal is best characterized by the sentence: *Please agree with me.* With this objective the speaker asserts the truth or wisdom of an opinion or belief. Through his demand, he uses—or at least implies —such verbs as *accept, affirm, approve, admit, believe, concede, recognize*—or *reject.* Note that the speaker asks for no more than mental agreement, a *covert* response. Some typical propositions are:

1. Castro is a threat to the United States.
2. The policy of the United States in Southeast Asia has failed.
3. The United Nations is exercising a positive force for peace.
4. The Girl Scouts need more support.
5. Many needy students are denied the opportunity to go to college.

Fig. 10.2. Do you persuade and convince? The adroit speaker must persuade a reluctant audience.

The Actuating Goal

This goal may be characterized by the sentence: *Please do as I recommend.* With this goal, the speaker seeks action, an *overt* response. Going one step beyond the convincing goal, he wants to push the listeners from the ranks of nonparticipants and neutrals into the rank of the active workers. The process would be:

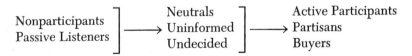

Nonparticipants Passive Listeners ⟶ Neutrals Uninformed Undecided ⟶ Active Participants Partisans Buyers

The speaker frames his proposition with the auxiliary *should* or *ought* plus a verb such as *buy, contribute, donate, support, write, join, vote.* This goal is the motive force in back of the salesman, the campaigner, the labor organizer, and the revivalist. Below are some typical recommending propositions.

1. You should install seat belts in your automobile.
2. You should help save the redwoods.
3. You should donate regularly to your church.
4. You should vote for John Smith.
5. You should join the English Speaking Union.
6. You should use a credit card.
7. You should organize an investment club.

STUDY YOUR LISTENERS

In Chapter IX, we discussed studying the listeners in order to determine what to include in the informative talk. In that context, you learned that the significant question is, "How much do the listeners know about the subject?"

In contrast to the informative talk, the speaker needs a different kind of information to prepare the persuasive speech. He wants to know how his listeners stand on the propostion, or whether they are for or against his stand.

On social and political issues, listeners vary in their *states of readiness* to act, falling somewhere along the following continuum:

Opposed	Undecided	Favorable
−4 −3 −2	−1 0 +1	+2 +3 +4

Because of previous associations, past experience, and education, they may be concentrated in a significant percentage somewhere along the scale. What does *significant percentage* mean? The answer is found in the question mark in the following:

$$\text{Supporters} + ? = 51\% \text{ or more}$$

What you fill in for the question mark will be the *significant percentage,* the number that you need to accomplish your goal. *This group is your target group,* the segment on which you should concentrate major effort.

To help you achieve your goal, you should ask yourself the following questions.

Fig. 10.3. Barry Goldwater often accomplished his persuasive goals with many of his listeners.

1. How are my listeners distributed on an attitude scale (in terms of their states of readiness)?
2. What percentage are favorable, neutral, and opposed to my proposition?
3. What segment holds the balance of power?
4. Do the listeners possess any favorable attitudes toward my position?
   a. Are these habitual or casual attitudes?
   b. How intense are these attitudes?
5. Do the listeners possess any unfavorable attitudes toward my position?
   a. Are these habitual or casual attitudes?
   b. How intense are these attitudes?
6. What percentage of the listeners must I win to achieve my final objective?

7. What is my target group?
8. Shall I seek to win individuals or shall I seek to win a group commitment?
9. Shall I demand an immediate response or a delayed response?
10. What type of materials must I use to achieve my goal?
11. If I concentrate upon a target group how shall I cope with the remainder of my listeners?

PLANNING YOUR STRATEGY

Back of every successful persuasive speech is a carefully conceived plan, a strategy of how to accomplish your desired goal with the given audience. As a purposeful speaker, you know what you want to accomplish. *The important question* is how far can you move as many listeners as possible toward your position; that is, how can you gain mental agreement and participation? Think of this problem on the basis of scale of ten:

Disagreement Opposition Inactivity			Mental Agreement				Enthusiastic Participation		
1	2	3	4	5	6	7	8	9	10

What kind of score can you hope to achieve in moving listeners from the position of opposition, inactivity and disinterest to the ranks of the enthusiastic participants (10)? When you encounter stiff resistance, you may find it necessary to give two or more speeches to convert sufficient members to ensure success. In this event, you need to select an immediate limited goal for each speech and a final objective for the series, as the following diagram suggests:

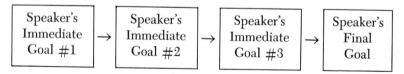

| Speaker's Immediate Goal #1 | → | Speaker's Immediate Goal #2 | → | Speaker's Immediate Goal #3 | → | Speaker's Final Goal |

Selecting a Speech Goal

In the previous section it has been implied that sound strategy is to plan the speech in such a way as to gain response from the listeners. To achieve his objective, the speaker must be sensitive to the attitudes of his listeners upon the subject that he is discussing. He must select his speech goal in terms of the position held by his target group. The two columns below illustrate how the position of the target group (on the left) dictates the type of goal (on the right) that the speaker chooses. Following these two columns is a practical example of how a speaker might translate these goals into four propositions.

POSITION OF TARGET GROUP	TYPE OF GOAL
Opponents—intense. Deep-seated opposition with more than 50% in this group.	Deliver stimulating speech on favorable attitude and develop common ground in order to disarm and weaken unfavorable attitudes.
Opponents—moderate. With large number of neutral listeners; and with small number of partisans.	Deliver a convincing speech, asking for mental agreement on main proposition or upon subproposition only when number of opponents is greater.
Neutrals—passive, undecided, uninformed, uninterested. With sufficient number when added to partisans to give you control; weak opponents.	Deliver actuating talk, asking for action on main proposition.
Partisans—lukewarm but not in agreement as to best solution. With almost enough to control the group, but with many undecided, and weak opponents.	Deliver actuating talk, making strong appeal for your solution.
Partisans—fully committed. With well over 50% in partisan group; with substantial number of neutrals, and only a small number in the opposition.	Stimulating speech, urging enthusiasm and fervor in completing the solution.

Now for illustrative purposes let us translate these three immediate goals into a series of four, interrelated propositions on a given

Fig. 10.4. In persuasion, it is important first to select carefully a speech goal in terms of your listeners' attitudes.

subject designed to move the listeners step by step toward the speaker's position. Acceptance of each one brings the listeners one step closer to successful promotion of the speaker's cause.

Stimulating: reinforcement of favorable attitudes.
    Proposition: It is more blessed to give than to receive.
Convincing: asking for mental agreement.
    Proposition: The Salvation Army helps the destitute.
Actuating: demand for action.
    Proposition: Give 10 dollars today to the Salvation Army.
Stimulating: stir enthusiasm.
    Proposition: Workers for the Salvation Army are "the salt of the earth."

These four propositions could serve for four talks or they could become subpoints in a single speech.

PUTTING YOUR DEMAND INTO A PROPOSITION

Already in Chapter III we have discussed how to organize a persuasive talk. Once you have studied your listeners carefully and decided upon a strategy, you are ready to frame your proposition.

You should put your demand into one single, simple, declarative sentence. In this sentence, you should express the whole message you want to put over.

If you have decided on stimulating or convincing goal you phrase an assertive proposition.

If you have decided upon an actuating speech, you phrase a recommending proposition proposing a course of action to be followed. For example, "You should buy. . . ."; "You should vote. . . ."; "You should refuse to pay. . . ."

MAKING SOUND REASONS PERSUASIVE

The title of this section implies that you have partitioned your proposition (see Chapter III) and have determined the points to support your proposal. But sound reasons, like good judgment, are often elusive. Of course, you cannot assume that merely connecting two thoughts (sentences) by the words *for* or *because* is an infallible sign of a logical relationship. What sometimes is suggested as a supporting point is no more than a rewording of the proposition or another point or even an unrelated statement.

Sound reasons come with effort. Wishing and dreaming will not produce them, nor are they fostered by intuition, whim, or rationalization. They are developed by extensive investigation, careful analysis and synthesis, and endless testing. They come from "the world as it really is"; they are consistent with other good reasons and with what recognized authorities consider to be sensible, realistic, expedient, and desirable.

But sound reasons worded in a cold, terse, impersonal form will not hit their mark; they will not touch or stir your listeners. For you

Fig. 10.5. Governor Mark Hatfield demonstrates "go-power."

to carry the day, your reasons must have what the television commercial calls "go-power"; they need the authority to arouse motives, to create desire, to make the listeners want to march. This so-called "go-power" comes through careful wording.

Here are five suggestions for wording points:

1. Keep the point simple and direct. Put it in the active voice in a short declarative or question form.
2. Give the point memory value. Choose language to help the listener remember it.
3. Word each point from the same view. If you speak in the second person in the first main point, use a similar subject in subsequent points.

4. Make each point tell the listener *why* he should agree with you or act upon your proposal.
5. Pack a motive appeal into each point.

Remember that "go-power" depends upon wording your points for your listeners. Below is illustrated how you may load impersonal points with motive appeals. The proposition is "Vote 'yes' on the increased tax levy":

IMPERSONAL POINTS	POINTS WITH MOTIVE APPEAL
First, the city needs more revenue for schools.	First, your favorable vote means a better education for our children.
Second, the city needs more revenue for law enforcement.	Second, your favorable vote means better police protection in the residential areas.
Third, the city needs more revenue for drainage.	Third, your favorable vote means prevention of floods in new residential areas.
Fourth, the city needs more revenue for sewage disposal.	Fourth, your favorable vote means elimination of the danger of a typhoid epidemic.

Substantiate Your Reasons With Supporting Materials

It is as important to put "go-power" in your supporting materials as well as in your points. When it stands alone, a point is no more than an assertion. Your listeners should ask you "for the facts," meaning that they deserve to have illustrations, examples, and statistics. Carefully review ways to put supporting materials in more meaningful form. Here are five suggestions:

1. By giving its source—provided it is a good one—you add persuasiveness to supporting material.
2. You must make your supporting material simple enough to be understood; complicated charts, long lists of statistics, and involved calculations are likely to frighten away your listeners.
3. You should select supporting materials that are representative of the large classes or groups of facts from which they are taken.
4. In the process of making material persuasive, you should not violate the total context from which it is drawn. In other words,

Fig. 10.6. To develop a cogent supporting argument it is necessary to do adequate research.

    you must not imply meanings which the original source did not intend.

5. You must make it clear that the evidence supports the point being proved and backs up your assertions.

    Here is a brief example of supporting material:

Assertion:	You should drive more carefully at night.
Source:	The National Safety Council tell us that
First fact:	three out of five traffic accidents occur at night when fewer persons are actually driving.
Second fact:	Night doubles traffic troubles. In cities the mileage rate of death per million miles jumps from 3 in the daytime to 6 after dark; and from 3 to 13 in the
Third fact:	country and small towns. Consider that when you are driving at 70 miles per hour at night, you need over 500 feet or about 33 car lengths to stop—a distance actually beyond your headlight range.

Conclusion: Driving at night is like driving in another world; to continue to push your car the way you do in the daytime is as silly as wearing summer clothes when it is twenty below.

A more detailed illustration follows in the form of a two-minute speech:

A TWO-MINUTE PERSUASIVE SPEECH

Beware of the Ladies

INTRODUCTION

Each year between May 15 and November 15 several seductive females blow into the Gulf area from the Caribbean. Before arriving they generally play around for a while in the West Indies. Their arrivals are well announced. We show our familiarity with these wanton ladies by calling them by their first names. In fact we laugh because they come in alphabetical order.

DEVELOPMENT

Problem: Now their names may amuse us, but make no mistake, these female hurricanes deserve your respect. Let me be more specific.

In 1900, a hurricane killed 6,000 persons and left 36,000 homeless in Galveston, Texas, just a few miles south of Louisiana. Ancient history, you say.

In 1955, Diane took 400 lives along the east coast.

In 1957, Audrey swept away 430 lives and millions of dollars of property in Louisiana and Texas.

In 1960, Donna killed 148 along the Atlantic seaboard.

In 1961, Carla claimed 40 lives in Texas.

In 1964, Hilda drove 150,000 Louisianians from their homes.

These wily seducers strike at speeds of 75 to 250 miles per hour, bringing with them equally vicious companions: heavy rain, thunder, lightning, and sometimes tidal waves. And not far behind are death and destruction.

Solution: When you hear a hurricane warning, remember the lady demon with the lovely name deserves your respect. Don't wait. Find cover. If you have a solid brick home, on high ground, away from the beach, stay inside and away from windows. But if your house is a wooden structure or in an area where flooding occurs, seek the protection in a nearby school or church of solid construction.

Don't dismiss the danger too soon, for the lady may turn around and strike you again full blast. Stay tuned in to your local TV or radio station until you hear the final all-clear.

CONCLUSION

Appeal: Be alert for the hurricane parade. Let me repeat the following advice: Don't wait! Stay inside for the final all-clear!

ETHOS IS POWERFUL

As we have already suggested in Chapter V, Aristotle gives a simple answer to those who search for the tricks of persuasion. He recommends that they look to their credibility. Once your listeners believe in your trustworthiness, your good will toward them, and and your expertness, the problems of changing belief and stirring action are lessened. You will be assured of greater attention and greater receptivity. In this sense, Christ was the greatest persuader of all times: Today, 900 million follow Him, and He is universally revered. It was through the power of his tremendous ethos that he moved men so dramatically to commitment and action.

Notice how Dr. Josef Kalvoda establishes his ethos in a speech he delivered at Mills College in 1963:

Good will,   Instead of telling you a few jokes at the beginning, as
   reverence for   it is customary, allow me to be unorthodox and to
   concepts   say something about myself. I am prejudiced on be-
   important   half of freedom of thought, speech, assembly and all
   to listeners: the other freedoms which we take here in the United
                      States for granted. I have a special reason to be fond
First reference   of liberty, because I have lost it already twice in the
   to first-hand   course of my life. I was born in Czechoslovakia
   experience: where we also took liberty for granted until the

Fig. 10.7. In addition to his marked speaking ability, Dr. Martin Luther King most often addresses an audience strongly motivated toward affirmative response.

political unit collapsed in 1938–1939. From then on, until 1945, I lived under Nazi totalitarianism. The three years following the end of the Second World War were an interlude of a semi-freedom that came to an end with the imposition of a new, Communist, totalitarianism.

Second reference to first-hand experience:

The idea of freedom may not be as real to most of you, who have never lived without it, and who have never lost it, as it is to one who experienced the dread chill of totalitarian terror and the life in Communist prison camps, who had to risk his life in

Third reference to first-hand experience:

*Fourth reference
to first-hand
experience:*

fleeing his native country in order to be free again. Liberty has a special meaning to one who roamed through foreign cities and foreign countries as a man without home, without a country, until the Statue of Liberty welcomed him to the New World.

*Fifth reference
to first-hand
experience:*

I was broke when I arrived here; but in this country of opportunity and individual freedom one can work and improve one's own position. I am very fond of this great country that gave me the opportunity to become a free man again, and to continue the struggle for freedom in the intellectual field that is certainly at least as important as that in the military, political or economic spheres.[1]

In this paragraph, Dr. Kalvoda carefully interweaves ethical and emotional appeals. Let us review the five instances he cites to establish that he has a right to speak on his subject because he has had first-hand experience with the loss and regaining of freedom:

He lived "under Nazi totalitarianism."
He lived under "new, Community, totalitarianism."
He "had to risk his life in fleeing his native country in order to be free again."
He "roamed through foreign cities and foreign countries as a man without a home, without a country. . . ."
"This country . . . gave me the opportunity to become a free man again."

He demonstrates his good will toward his listeners by expressing reverence for what his listeners revere: "I am prejudiced on behalf of freedom of thought, speech, assembly and all the other freedoms." Later he says, "I am very fond of this great country."

Of course, the paragraph is also packed with several motive appeals: appeals to self preservation, self esteem, and patriotism.

[1] Josef Kalvoda, "Academic Freedom in the Age of Conflict," *Vital Speeches of the Day,* **29** (June 15, 1963), pp. 526–527.

STIRRING THE LISTENERS' MOTIVES

Vance Packard recently wrote two best sellers, *The Hidden Persuaders* (1957) and *The Status Seekers* (1959), that fascinated, amazed, and frightened millions of Americans. Packard made us aware of *motive appeals*. Now, it was permissible for this skillful writer to imply that his subject was "strange and rather exotic" but certainly it was not new; it had been known since the time of Aristotle and before. Packard mainly dealt with how advertisers use motives to make consumers susceptible to persuasion.

Packard reports on an executive who observed "that women will pay two dollars and a half for skin cream but no more than twenty-five cents for a cake of soap." The executive added, "The women are buying a promise. . . . The cosmetic manufacturers are not selling lanolin, they are selling hope. . . . We no longer buy oranges, we buy vitality. We do not buy just an auto, we buy prestige."[2]

Yes, we all buy *hope, vitality,* and *prestige* many times. These and other desires are internal compulsions which stir us to action. No one needs to tell you when you should eat or drink; the signs are well known to you. And when anything stands in your way to satisfy these cravings, you become unhappy and begin to look for ways to solve the problems. These physiological drives (desires, or wants) and other similar ones become more complex through social conditioning and experience. They manifest themselves in a variety of ways. As speakers, you can release or stir up these compulsions, or springs of action, which we shall henceforth refer to as *motive appeals.*

Seven Motive Appeals

There are seven motive appeals which exert strong influence on human thought and behavior:

1. Self-preservation: The desire to protect oneself or material well-being:

[2] Vance Packard, *The Hidden Persuaders,* McKay, 1957, p. 8.

The idea of freedom may not be as real to most of you . . . as it is to one who experienced the dread chill of totalitarian terror and the life in Communist prison camps, who had to risk his life in fleeing his native country. . . .

We must fight to keep our party out of the hands of the extremists on the right as well as on the left.

2. Self-esteem: pride in accomplishment or feeling of personal worth:

If your son or daughter graduates from State University you are to be congratulated.

Building your own sailboat will give you a real sense of accomplishment.

3. Acquisitiveness: the desire for ownership or material possessions:

Why take less! Invest your money with us and earn a full eight per cent each year.

Our endowment policy will give you a substantial income when you are fifty years old.

4. Belongingness: loyalty to group, family, or state:

Why are thousands demanding each day our new drink Zillo?

Frenchmen! For more than thirty years in peace and war I have marched with you, and I am marching still along the same road (*Winston Churchill*).

We all belong within the grand old Republican party.

5. Social approval: the desire for status and recognition:

All the smart set are joining our Music Lovers Society.

Exclusive subdivision. All houses are in $50,000 to $100,000 range. Here you can live in luxurious comfort with selected neighbors, near a country club.

6. Exploration: the desire for adventure; the lure of the unknown:

Shipmates wanted to join a beautiful sailing cruise for lazy vacation of beachcombing through the South Seas.

Dining at the Two Candle Inn is filled with unforgettable delight.

7. Aesthetic enjoyment: appreciation of beauty:

For an evening of relaxation attend the concert of the Symphony Orchestra at the City Auditorium.

Here is a truly wonderful selection of classical recordings that belongs in any collection.

Set your table with the finest silver.

The names given to the seven motives may not please you. You perhaps have another set of names, or you may wish to add several others. Further, careful analysis of the above list will reveal overlapping. In making this discovery, you have stumbled onto a valuable principle: Motives are difficult to classify and affect different persons in different ways.

Some Suggestions For Using Motives

In order to make effective use of motive appeals within a speech, you consider the following five principles:

1. Direct your appeals to more than one motive; they will vary in strength with different persons and at different times.
2. Avoid naming the motives; work them into the speech without calling attention to them.
3. Don't overwork any one appeal or group of appeals; attempt to include a variety of appeals.
4. Be sure that the satisfying of the motive is not beyond the listener.
5. Combine the motive appeals with logical appeals.
6. Keep your appeals on a high plane; work on the socially oriented appeals (altruistic) whenever possible.

MAKING ACCEPTANCE EASY FOR YOUR LISTENERS

George Brown delivered a stirring appeal to donate blood to the blood bank. He pointed out how there was a desperate local shortage for certain rare types. He actually cited several instances of personal acquaintances who had found themselves needing blood for transfusions. He was particularly effective when he described a five-year-old whose life depended upon daily transfusions. In concluding, he simply said, "you can donate blood at any hospital." *This talk failed.* After a terrific build up, Brown failed to make response easy for his listeners. His listeners were confused and puzzled as to how to help. What could he have done? Any or all of the following would have improved his chances of success:

1. He could have given the exact location of the three local agencies prepared to received blood donations.
2. He could have given the telephone number and hours when the centers were open.
3. He could have placed this information upon a card to hand each listener for later reference.
4. He could have offered to arrange appointments for interested persons.
5. He could have offered to provide transportation for those who wanted to go.
6. He could have assured his listeners that donating blood is not painful or dangerous.
7. He could have volunteered to accompany any person who was afraid.
8. He could have made his proposal a group project in order that donors would feel a sense of belonging and not feel that they were alone in their giving.
9. He could have prepared some kind of recognition or award for those who donated.

Your listeners are not likely to respond to your requests when they must overcome obstacles to carry out your proposal, or when responding is embarrassing. Firmly set in their habits, they are likely to resist change, the unfamiliar, the embarrassing, and what they do not understand. They will find it easier to do nothing and to remain anonymous. Below are some specific suggestions about gaining the acceptance of your proposition:

1. Your proposal should be specific in its details; it must give time, place, how much, etc.
2. Your request must appear to the listener to be a reasonable one; it must not request more than listeners can give.
3. Your request should provide for or at least produce immediate

satisfaction; rewards in heaven are too remote or too far off for most of us.

4. Your request should bring satisfaction and pleasure; it should offer a "plausible way" for your hearers "to save their faces when they change courses or withdraw from a stand they have taken."[3]

5. Your request should require a minimum of physical, mental, or emotional effort.

MOVE FROM AGREEMENT TO DISAGREEMENT

How do you listen to television? If you are like millions of other Americans, when you hear something with which you disagree, you tune in another channel. You engage in "self-protective exercises" of selective exposure, selective perception, and selective retention. Joseph Klapper observes that when listeners encounter unsympathetic material, "they often seem not to perceive it, or to recast and interpret it to fit their existing views or to forget it more readily than they forget sympathetic material."[4]

What does selective listening have to do with the oral persuader? It points up clearly the necessity for maintaining attention, interest, and sympathetic listening to the very end, to the necessity of moving from common ground into areas involving changes of opinion and behavior. The speaker who, in the beginning, censures and criticizes moral conduct, who violates the taboos and mores, who challenges cherished institutions or ideals is likely to lose his hearers before he moves into the heart of his speech.

Let us enumerate ten steps showing a possible method for moving toward adoption:

1. Gain initial attention
2. Express a conciliatory attitude and respect for opposition
3. Stress common ground and common feelings which he has with listeners
4. Strengthen related attitudes favorable to his position and weaken attitudes unfavorable

[3] James Winans, *Speech-Making*, Appleton-Century-Crofts, 1935, p. 317.
[4] Joseph T. Klapper, *The Effects of Mass Communication*, Free Press, 1960, p. 19.

5. Orient listeners with reference to the background and nature of problem
6. Develop the problem, showing how it hurts the welfare of listeners
7. Move to stronger arguments, touching more sensitive areas
8. Reveal solution to problem and give proposition
9. Show possible advantages to listeners
10. Make strong appeal for acceptance

The ten steps just listed are a fitting summary of this process of persuasion. They suggest that the speaker lead (not compel, coerce, or manipulate) his listeners successively through the following:

1. Attention
2. Acceptance
3. Adoption
4. Action

The process is not accidental or haphazard. It is carefully conceived and thoughtfully modified to cope with changing moods. It is gradual, with each new step built upon the one before. It progresses at a rate determined by the listener's willingness to respond.

Being persuasive involves moving the listeners from where you find them to where you want them.

QUESTIONS FOR INVESTIGATION AND DISCUSSION

1. What is persuasion? Be sure to check the writings of social psychologists and public-opinion experts as well as speech teachers.
2. In what ways do the following terms differ: *persuasion, conviction, propaganda,* and *brainwashing?*
3. What justification is there for the view that all speeches, regardless of type, have action as a goal?
4. Under what circumstances is persuasion unethical?

Fig 10.8. The significant occasion, the beautiful setting and the effective speech together become a long-remembered experience.

5. How is preparation of a persuasive speech different from the preparation of an informative speech?
6. What are the differences between the informative and the persuasive speech in terms of analysis, central thought, organization, and supporting material?
7. What are the differences in audience analysis for the informative and the persuasive speech?
8. Why must a proposition for a persuasive speech be worded in a complete sentence?

9. What are several other names for motive appeals?
10. When is it unethical to appeal to motives?
11. Are logical appeals and motive appeals mutually exclusive? Find examples to support your answer.
12. Define the following: (1) emotionally loaded language; (2) report language; (3) signal response; (4) symbol response; (5) denotative meaning; (6) connotative meaning. See Winston L. Brembeck and William Smiley Howell, *Persuasion: A Means of Social Control*, Prentice-Hall, 1952, chap. IX.
13. Is it "ethical" to move from areas of agreement toward areas of disagreement? Support your answer.
14. What personality traits are associated with the successful persuasive speaker?
15. What are the differences between simplification to make clear and simplification to persuade? Under what circumstances are these practices unethical?

ASSIGNMENTS

CLASS PROJECT

1. *Impromptu phase:* A class committee of three will prepare a list of 30 topics on the general theme. Each topic will be phrased in question form. In class—when his turn to speak comes—each member of the class will be permitted to draw three topics. He will put two back into receptacle and speak on the third for not more than three minutes.

2. *Manuscript phase:* Each member of the class will prepare a manuscript speech of no more than 800 words on some aspect of the general theme. This speech should be carefully polished and rehearsed. It may be presented either from manuscript or from complete memory.

3. *Group evaluation:* Each member of the class will evaluate other class members. If you have had groups, use a *rank order*, ranking the members from 1 through 6. If you have not divided into subgroups, then rate the members of the class on the basis of five categories: superior, excellent, average, fair, poor.

SPEAKING ASSIGNMENTS

1. Plan a series of three, five-minute speeches on a single theme, making the first stimulating; the second convincing; and the third actuating.

2. Deliver a five-minute sales talk on some useful product. Build the talk around a demonstration.

3. Deliver an actuating talk in which you seek an overt response (for example, donating to a good cause). Be sure to make acceptance easy for the listeners.

RESEARCH ASSIGNMENTS

1. Find an advertisement in which the following five steps are present: introduction, problem, solution, benefits, and appeal.

2. Analyze the motive appeals in a full-page magazine advertisement.

3. Collect several lists of motive appeals and classify the names under five to seven common headings. Compare your list with those of other members of the class.

4. Prepare a written analysis of the motive appeals found in Adlai Stevenson's "Eulogy of Eleanor Roosevelt," found in the Appendix. You should also study Mr. Stevenson's careful choice of language, noticing how he achieves his effect with simple words.

BULLETIN BOARD ASSIGNMENT

Theme: Persuaders in Action.

SUGGESTED READINGS

Braden, Waldo W., and Earnest Brandenburg, *Oral Decision-Making*, Harper & Row, 1955, chap. 23.

Brembeck, Winston Lamont, and William Smiley Howell, *Persuasion: A Means of Social Control*, Prentice-Hall, 1952.

Brigance, William Norwood, *Speech: Its Techniques and Disciplines in a Free Society* (2nd ed.), Appleton-Century-Crofts, 1961, chap. 7.

Bryant, Donald C., and Karl R. Wallace, *Fundamentals of Public Speaking* (3rd ed.), Appleton-Century-Crofts, 1960, Part VI. This section is composed of seven excellent chapters dealing with audience analysis, suggestion, analysis, and planning.

Gray, Giles Wilkeson, and Waldo W. Braden, *Public Speaking: Principles and Practice* (2nd ed.), Harper & Row, 1963, chaps. 9, 10, 20, and 21.

Thonssen, Lester, and A. Craig Baird, *Speech Criticism*, Ronald, 1948, chaps. 11, 12, and 13.

✿✿✿✿✿✿ APPENDIX

THREE SPECIMEN SPEECHES

BY JOHN A. GRONOUSKI[1]

MAIL SERVICE

I would like to begin with a statistic. Starting right now, and in less time than it takes for me to talk to you tonight, post offices across the country will have processed one and a half million pieces of mail! That is a rough estimate. But it should give you some idea of the hugeness of the operation I have been charged with conducting for the past year. Permit me to stagger you with a few more statistics:

[1] Delivered at Milwaukee Chapter, Association of Industrial Advertisers, Milwaukee, Wisconsin, September 10, 1964; *Vital Speeches of the Day,* **XXX** (October 1, 1964), 755–757. Used by permission.

The Post Office has 590,000 employees. We are the largest civilian agency in government, and we operate the most far-flung communications system in the world. Our budget is $5 billion annually. We own or rent more than 100,000 vehicles in some 44,000 post offices, branches, stations, garages, and other buildings. Our 150,000 letter carriers each day travel seven times the distance covered by Astronaut John Glenn in his three orbits around the earth.

Congress has also assigned us some extra-curricular chores. We register aliens, count livestock, issue bird hunting permits, deliver books for the blind, sell small boat stamps for the Coast Guard, distribute federal tax forms, sell property transfer stamps, conduct Civil Service examinations, supply information about the Peace Corps, report forest fires and handle forms for the census.

In our spare time we also sell commemorative stamps.

One of our most vital functions lies in the area of law enforcement. In the 12 months ending last June 30, our Postal Inspectors conducted a total of 112,956 criminal investigations—ranging from mail fraud to pornography. During that year 12,006 arrests were made and the Inspection Service helped to secure 10,485 convictions. Of all the cases brought to trial, 99 per cent resulted in convictions. This is a record unbeaten by any other law enforcement agency—federal, state or local.

The Post Office Department also has cooperated fully with President Johnson's Committee on Consumer Interests. Our Chief Inspector, Henry Montague, is my personal representative on the Committee headed by Mrs. Esther Peterson. We are giving particular attention to protecting the public—especially our senior citizens—against mail fraud swindles involving land offered for vacation or retirement.

We are proud of the job our postal inspectors are doing. And we are proud of our postal personnel—for their dedication to duty, for their loyalty, and for their perseverance in carrying out the myriad responsibilities entrusted to them.

Diversity is a characteristic of the Post Office Department. So is growth. In 1933 each person in the United States averaged 158 letters a year. Today the annual average is more than 360—or one a day for each person, with a couple of spares for a quiet Sunday afternoon.

You and I appreciate, of course, that while this is a national average it doesn't mean that every person in the country sits down and writes a letter every day in the week. Fully 75 per cent of the total mail volume is generated by business and commercial interests, and another 15 per cent is *inspired* by business. For example, over 90 per cent of all insurance business is transacted by mail. It wouldn't surprise me if the advertising industry percentage is as high—or maybe even higher.

Third class mail, which is mostly advertising material, accounts for an estimated thirty billion dollars in annual sales and provides jobs for from four to five million Americans.

And it is a major part of an annual mail volume that this year is expected to total 72 billion pieces. With each passing year, the volume grows—at the rate of more than two billion pieces a year. Annually, we add to our delivery system one and a half million city addresses, 100,000 rural addresses and 75,000 business addresses.

Our problem is to cope with this rising volume of mail without:

1. Putting a bigger dent in the budget. Or
2. Raising postal rates.

This is the problem. This is the challenge.

We think we have faced up to that challenge. President Johnson has instructed all federal agencies "to give a dollar's worth of value for a dollar spent." We have complied with that directive. We have economized to the bone, without cutting essential services.

We have established a rapport with our employee organizations that has enabled us to reach a peak of productivity unequaled in the history of the Department.

Modern electronic addressing and mailing equipment breeds much of the increased mail volume we must handle now and in the future. We have learned to use mechanization to help us handle this avalanche of mail. We have installed proven mechanized equipment in our larger offices where it has demonstrated its value in helping our personnel. And we are in the process of training our people for new skills so that they can operate the machinery we are installing.

But mechanization is not the sole answer to our problems. We have also developed advanced techniques in management to keep abreast of our growth in volume.

The postal service is a lively and flexible business that provides service daily to each of our more than 192 million citizens. It is an operation where change is the rule rather than the exception, and the unpredictable a daily event rather than the expected.

Permit me to give you some specifics about what we are doing, and what we expect to do.

Early in this Administration, it was determined by the Post Office Department that the business community and the postal system had a common interest and a meeting ground—75 per cent of all mail is business mail.

In an outstanding example of free enterprise and federal government cooperation, we established the Nationwide Improved Mail Service program, called NIMS. Mail Users Councils, consisting of some 20,000 top mailers in more than 300 communities, were organized throughout the 50 states.

Their immediate goal: To work with postal experts in reducing the avalanche of mail which descended on our post offices after five in the evening, jamming our equipment, slowing our handling capability, and causing millions of important items to miss early train and plane connections.

By spreading their mail deposits over the day—instead of dumping it all on the post office in one load, late in the day—these mailers reduced our after-five "peak load" from 80 per cent of the day's mail volume to about 50 per cent.

The result is that we are better able to schedule our work force throughout the day, night differential is considerably reduced, and machinery which was previously idle up to 18 hours a day may now be utilized on a more regular basis.

The postal establishment and the business community also developed the Accelerated Business Collection and Delivery program—called ABCD for short.

This is perhaps the most dramatic example I can cite of the effectiveness of this era of business-government cooperation.

Today, in 271 cities—including Milwaukee—letters mailed in the business district by 11 A.M., in specified boxes, are delivered within the same district by 3 o'clock that afternoon. Four-hour delivery service is guaranteed!

As a result of the ABCD program, first-day delivery is provided for more American mail than for all the mail in the rest of the world combined! This program is a vital first step in our long-sought goal of making available next-day delivery in any part of the country.

NIMS and ABCD represent steps we are taking to deal with the burgeoning mail volume—steps through which we can prevent an explosive rise in manpower, while at the same time improving service.

Another such step—and one we made with 20-league boots—is the ZIP Code program—the most vital advance in mail processing since the start of city delivery service a hundred years ago.

I'm sure you are all familiar with Mr. ZIP and his five little digits, by now—and I sincerely hope you are all using it. Because, if you're not, you're out of step with the times.

Basically, ZIP Code is a five-numeral routing system which permits mail to be sorted to 566 sectional centers, and thence to the destination point, bypassing many handlings and leap-frogging over many bottlenecks between the point of mailing and the point of delivery.

The first three digits of the number represent the sectional center— and the last two digits are comparable to the old zone numbers used in many cities since World War II.

A sectional center is a mail concentration point, selected because its physical location makes it a focal point for air, highway and rail transportation.

These transportation focal points—these sectional centers—make up the backbone of the ZIP Code program.

When large-volume mailers presort their mail by ZIP Code, and deliver it to the sectional center nearest the point of origin, their mail "leap-frogs" from sectional center to sectional center, eliminating a number of manual handlings along the way, which, of necessity, used to detain their mail en route.

This saves the Post Office Department money, speeds the mails, and cuts down on the possibility of error. It enables us to keep pace with the great and growing volume of mail—to move it with a minimum of expense and a maximum of efficiency—thus forestalling the day when postage rates might otherwise have to be increased.

I predict that ten years from now every major shipper in the country will be patterning its routing system on our sectional center concept.

And such a development will be born of necessity.

The day when every town in America of any size had a train coming through—or one passing through an adjacent city—has long since passed.

Thirty years ago, some 10,000 trains served virtually every city and town in the United States. Today, the number of trains in operation has declined to about 1,200. Their schedules have been drastically curtailed, and many areas of our country are completely inaccessible by rail.

ZIP Code is also applicable to parcel post, with the result that damage to parcels is considerable decreased.

Here's an example.

In Philadelphia, Pennsylvania, we have fully implemented ZIP Code distribution for outgoing parcel post.

Under this program, parcels bearing ZIP Code in their addresses are distributed *nationwide* to sectional centers nearest the address point.

Let me elucidate.

Say someone in Philadelphia was mailing a package to someone in Lakewood, Wisconsin, in the pre-ZIP Code days.

That package would be distributed at Philadelphia to a sack labeled "Chicago, Illinois—Wisconsin Parcel Post." It would then have to go through another distribution system at Chicago, prior to being dispatched to Green Bay, Wisconsin, and then to Lakewood.

But today, if the package contained the Lakewood ZIP Code—54138—in its address, it would be sorted at Philadelphia directly to the Green Bay Sectional Center, to be put on the first transportation to nearby Lakewood.

This means less handling of every package—and less handling mean less likelihood of damage to packages in transit.

Another innovation which is calculated to reduce parcel damage is what we call the "pool case." This is a rigid card-board or plastic box container which mailers may use to consolidate all their parcels destined for a specific area of the country. The packages are pre-sorted directly into this box—or "pool case"—which is then sealed and travels, unopened, directly to its destination.

And still another area in which we are endeavoring to improve parcel post service is an experiment which began just this week in Annapolis, Maryland.

It is a venture in scheduled parcel post service .

If the tests prove successful—and we have reason to believe they will—you should be able to learn soon from your postmaster just when your parcels can be expected to reach their destination, provided the destination is within given geographical limits.

In a great many cases, the schedules will call for next day delivery of parcel post—and that will mean first-rate service for fourth class mail.

These steps which I have outlined to you today—steps to improve your mail service and to increase its capacity to serve all Americans —are as vital to today's postal system as was the post road to the fledgling mail program devised by Benjamin Franklin 200 years ago.

They are signs that we are, as President Johnson has urged us, keeping our eyes focused "not upon the needs of the past, but upon the accomplishments of the present and the promise of the future."

We in the Postal Service and you businessmen who generate so much of the mail we handle have a common goal and a mutual bond —the finest possible mail service at the lowest possible cost.

Together, we are achieving that objective.

BY ADLAI E. STEVENSON[1]

EULOGY OF
ELEANOR ROOSEVELT

One week ago this afternoon, in the Rose Garden at Hyde Park, Eleanor Roosevelt came home for the last time. Her journeys are over. The remembrance now begins.

In gathering here to honor her, we engage in a self-serving act. It is we who are trying, by this ceremony of tribute, to deny the fact that we have lost her, and, at least, to prolong the farewell, and

[1] Delivered at a memorial service at the Cathedral of St. John the Divine, New York City, November 17, 1962. Copy furnished by Mr. Stevenson. Used by permission.

—possibly—to say some of the things we dared not say in her presence, because she would have turned aside such testimonial with impatience and gently asked us to get on with some of the more serious business of the meeting.

A grief perhaps not equaled since the death of her husband seventeen years ago is the world's best tribute to one of the great figures of our age—a woman whose lucid and luminous faith testified always for sanity in an insane time and for hope in a time of obscure hope—a woman who spoke for the good toward which man aspires in a world which has seen too much of the evil of which man is capable.

She lived seventy-eight years, most of the time in tireless activity as if she knew that only a frail fragment of the things that cry out to be done could be done in the lifetime of even the most fortunate. One has the melancholy sense that when she knew death was at hand, she was contemplating not what she achieved, but what she had not quite managed to do. And I know she wanted to go—when there was no more strength to do.

Yet how much she had done—how much still unchronicled! We dare not try to tabulate the lives she salvaged, the battles—known and unrecorded—she fought, the afflicted she comforted, the hovels she brightened, the faces and places, near and far, that were given some new radiance, some sound of music, by her endeavors. What other single human being has touched and transformed the existence of so many others? What better measure is there of the impact of anyone's life?

There was no sick soul too wounded to engage her mercy. There was no signal of human distress which she did not view as a personal summons. There was no affront to human dignity from which she fled because the timid cried "danger." And the number of occasions on which her intervention turned despair into victory we may never know.

Her life was crowded, restless, fearless. Perhaps she pitied most not those whom she aided in the struggle, but the more fortunate who were preoccupied with themselves and cursed with the self-deceptions of private success. She walked in the slums and ghettos of the world, not on a tour of inspection, nor as a condescending patron, but as one who could not feel complacent while others were hungry, and who could not find contentment while others were in distress. This was not sacrifice; this, for Mrs. Roosevelt, was the only meaningful way of life.

These were not conventional missions of mercy. What rendered this unforgettable woman so extraordinary was not merely her response to suffering; it was her comprehension of the complexity of the human condition. Not long before she died, she wrote that "within all of us there are two sides. One reaches for the stars, the other descends to the level of beasts." It was, I think, this discernment that made her so unfailingly tolerant of friends who faltered, and led her so often to remind the smug and the complacent that "there but for the grace of God. . . ."

But we dare not regard her as just a benign incarnation of good works. For she was not only a great woman and a great humanitarian, but a great democrat. I use the word with a small "d"—though it was, of course, equally true that she was a great Democrat with a capital "D." When I say that she was a great small "d" democrat, I mean that she had a lively and astute understanding of the nature of the democratic process. She was a master political strategist with a fine sense of humor. And, as she said, she loved a good fight.

She was a realist. Her compassion did not become sentimentality. She understood that progress was a long labor of compromise. She mistrusted absolutism in all its forms—the absolutism of the word and even more the absolutism of the deed. She never supposed that all the problems of life could be cured in a day or a year or a lifetime. Her pungent and salty understanding of human behavior kept her always in intimate contact with reality. I think this was a primary source of her strength, because she never thought that the loss of a battle meant the loss of a war, nor did she suppose that a compromise which produced only part of the objective sought was an act of corruption or of treachery. She knew that no formula of words, no combination of deeds, could abolish the troubles of life overnight and usher in the millennium.

The miracle, I have tried to suggest, is how much tangible good she really did; how much realism and reason were mingled with her instinctive compassion; how her contempt for the perquisites of power ultimately won her the esteem of so many of the powerful; and how, at her death, there was a universality of grief that transcended all the harsh boundaries of political, racial and religious strife and, for a moment at least, united men in a vision of what their world might be.

We do not claim the right to enshrine another mortal, and this least of all would Mrs. Roosevelt have desired. She would have wanted it said, I believe, that she well knew the pressures of pride and vanity, the sting of bitterness and defeat, the gray days of national peril and personal anguish. But she clung to the confident expectation that men could fashion their own tomorrows if they could only learn that yesterday can be neither relived or revised.

Many who have spoken of her in these last few days have used a word to which we all assent, because it speaks a part of what we feel. They have called her "a lady," a "great lady," "the first lady of the world." But the word "lady," though it says much about Eleanor Roosevelt, does not say all. To be incapable of self-concern is not a negative virtue; it is the other side of a coin that has a positive face— the most positive, I think, of all the faces. And to enhance the humanity of others is not a kind of humility; it is a kind of pride—the noblest of all the forms of pride. No man or woman can respect other men and women who do not respect life. And to respect life is to love it. Eleanor Roosevelt loved life—and that, perhaps, is the most meaningful thing that can be said about her, for it says so much beside.

It takes courage to love life. Loving it demands imagination and perception and the kind of patience women are more apt to have than men—the bravest and most understanding women. And loving it takes something more beside—it takes a gift for life, a gift for love.

Eleanor Roosevelt's childhood was unhappy—miserably unhappy, she sometimes said. But it was Eleanor Roosevelt who also said that "one must never, for whatever reason, turn his back on life." She did not mean that duty should compel us. She meant that life should. "Life," she said, "was meant to be lived." A simple statement. An obvious statement. But a statement that by its obviousness and its simplicity challenges the most intricate of all the philosophies of despair.

Many of the admonitions she bequeathed us are neither new thoughts nor novel concepts. Her ideas were, in many respects, old-fashioned—as old as the Sermon on the Mount, as the reminder that it is more blessed to give than to receive. In the words of St. Francis that she loved so well: "For it is in the giving that we receive."

She imparted to the familiar language—nay, what too many have come to treat as the clichés—of Christianity a new poignancy and vibrance. She did so not by reciting them, but by proving that it is possible to live them. It is this above all that rendered her unique in her century. It was said of her contemptuously at times that she was a *do-gooder*, a charge leveled with similar derision against another public figure 1,962 years ago.

We who are assembled here are of various religious and political faiths, and perhaps different conceptions of man's destiny in the universe. It is not an irreverence, I trust, to say that the immortality Mrs. Roosevelt would have valued most would be found in the deeds and visions her life inspired in others, and in the proof that they would be faithful to the spirit of any tribute conducted in her name.

And now one can almost hear Mrs. Roosevelt saying that the speaker has already talked too long. So we must say farewell. We are always saying farewell in this world—always standing at the edge of loss attempting to retrieve some memory, some human meaning, from the silence—something which was precious and is gone.

Often, although we know the absence well enough, we cannot name it or describe it even. What left the world when Lincoln died? Speaker after speaker in those aching days tried to tell his family or his neighbors or his congregation. But no one found the words, not even Whitman. "When lilacs last in the dooryard bloomed" can break the heart, but not with Lincoln's greatness, only with his loss. What the words could never capture was the man himself. His deeds were known; every school child knew them. But it was not his deeds the country mourned: it was the man—the mastery of life which made the greatness of the man.

It is always so. On that April day when Franklin Roosevelt died, it was not a President we wept for. It was a man. In Archibald MacLeish's words:

> "Fagged out, worn down, sick
> With the weight of his own bones,
> the task finished,
> The war won, the victory assured,

The glory left behind him for
            the others
(And the wheels roll up through
   the night in the sweet land
In the cool air in the spring
     between the lanterns)."[2]

It is so now. What we have lost in Eleanor Roosevelt is not her life. She lived that out to the full. What we have lost, what we wish to recall for ourselves, to remember, is what she was herself. And who can name it? But she left "a name to shine on the entablatures of truth, forever."

We pray that she has found peace, and a glimpse of sunset. But today we weep for ourselves. We are lonelier; someone has gone from one's own life—who was like the certainty of refuge; and someone has gone from the world—who was like a certainty of honor.

[2] Quoted by permission of Mr. Archibald MacLeish.

BY JAMES L. GOLDEN[1]

MOMENTS TO REMEMBER

I am happy to be here and participate in this memorable occasion despite the fact a few years ago Chancellor Samuel Gould of the University of California at Santa Barbara observed: "The commencement speaker represents the continuation of a barbaric custom that has no place in logic." Mr. Gould's derogatory view of a sacred tradition which spans more than two centuries has had little effect

[1] Delivered as a Commencement Address, at John Glenn High School, May 29, 1964; *Vital Speeches of the Day*, **XXX** (July 1, 1964), 570–572. Used by permission.

in altering the course of scholastic history. For this year's graduation exercises in the United States will feature approximately 30,000 commencement orators who will address the seniors of our colleges, universities, and secondary schools. Unfortunately the speaker and his speech will not long be remembered. Dr. Eugene S. Wilson, Dean of Admissions at Amherst College, questioned forty adults concerning their commencement speaker and his theme. Not one could remember either the name of the orator or the details of the address. One woman who at first was certain that her commencement speaker was a general, learned after a little research that he merely "had been an officer in the General Electric Company."

Despite this discouraging picture of the commencement speaker's effectiveness, I am going to ask you to have faith that what I say this evening will be both relevant and significant. It is not my purpose to remind you that in order to make a mark in life you must press forward, or stand upon a block of granite, or gaze upon a star, or climb though the rocks be rugged. Nor is it my aim to urge you to accept the "challenge of the sixties" or the "challenge of change." Instead of this traditional focus upon the future, I am going to ask you to relive with me the principal events which took place during your four years at John Glenn High School. It is my hope that these historical moments not only will tell you where you have been but will help inspire you to chart your future role in a dynamic and revolutionary world.

In the Fall of 1960 you were a group of fourteen-year-old freshmen who came to John Glenn excited about your new teachers and your projected courses in English, Math, General Science, Physical Education, Latin and Spanish. You thought of your new friends and your new environment as you asked the question: "What is high school really like?" The six hours which you spent here each day opened new areas of knowledge. But what was happening outside of the classroom perhaps provided you with your greatest moment to remember. Two attractive political leaders, both in their forties, were seeking the presidency. Out of New England came John Fitzgerald Kennedy, the youngest Democratic candidate of the twentieth century. With evangelical fervor and a virile style expressed in urgent tones, he pleaded with the American people to follow him to the "New Frontier." His opponent, the Vice President of the United States, Richard Milhaus Nixon, wended his way from his native California to the other forty nine states asking for an extension of the Eisenhower years. Through the television screens these articulate spokesmen of contemporary politics entered the living rooms of seventy million people, bringing them face to face with history in the making.

When the contest was over, a divided America had elected a new president by a razor-edge margin of one tenth of one per cent. A few months later John Kennedy was inaugurated the thirty-fifth President of the United States. We cannot soon forget the eloquent words which he spoke on that occasion.

"United there is little we cannot do . . .

Let us never negotiate out of fear. But let us never fear to negotiate.

Ask not what your country can do for you—Ask what you can do for your country.

Let the word go forth from this time and place, to friend and foe alike, that the torch has been passed to a new generation of Americans—born in this country, tempered by war, disciplined by a hard and bitter peace, proud of our ancient heritage."

The election of Mr. Kennedy constitutes a significant landmark in American history. For "he was," observes the *Washington Post,* "the first Roman Catholic and the first man born in the twentieth century to become President . . . and at forty-three the youngest man ever elected to that great office." This historical event which occurred during your freshman year speaks again to you on the night of your graduation, and this is what it says. Young men and women with courage, determination, and ambition can—despite handicaps and hardships—often ascend to the top of their chosen profession. Moreover, it says that the worth of a man shall no longer be measured by the yardstick of religious intolerance. As Mr. Kennedy himself so ably put it in his famous address before the Greater Houston Ministerial Association: "I believe in an America where religious intolerance will someday end—where all men and all churches are treated as equal—where every man has the same right to attend or not to attend the church of his choice."

As you moved into your sophomore year you anticipated such

new courses as World History, Biology, Plane Geometry, Geography, and Driver Education. You took pride in your increased maturity and sophistication; indeed, you even smiled in retrospect at your freshman eagerness and naïveté. Little did you realize that within a few months your school and your town would be thrust into national prominence. February 20, 1962 marked the date of your second great moment to remember. John Glenn, forty years of age, climbed into an instrument-packed capsule called Friendship 7 and waited for the countdown. As the numbers were sounded off, the residents of New Concord breathed hard, Times Square in New York stood still, and the Western World with a quickening pulse and heartbeat watched and prayed. Suddenly a shout of relief could be heard as Colonel Glenn, now heading into the radiant sky, uttered his first words: "Lift off. The clock is operating. We're underway."

For the next four hours and fifty-six minutes the man who was to give your school its name soared in space at 17,530 miles per hour. Ranging from 100 to 160 miles above the earth, he crossed the Atlantic, the continent of Africa, the Indian Ocean, Australia, the Pacific, and the United States. Every forty-five minutes he went from daylight to darkness and back again. In all he saw four beautiful sunsets in one day, experienced the exhilaration of weightlessness, and flirted with death during those agonizing moments of re-entry. "Were you very tense at take off?" Vice President Johnson asked him. "I imagine I was," Glenn replied. Said Johnson: "You were about as near the Lord's end as a person ever is."

But what is the relevance of John Glenn's flight to you tonight? Why should this feat stand as a moment to remember? First it towers majestically as a monument to the age of science. After centuries of frustration man had demonstrated at long last his ability to offset the law of gravity; he had proved that he could function in space with more accuracy than the robot mechanisms which might surround him. Equally important he had successfully set the stage for interplanetary travel which will soon take him to the moon. Secondly, it shows that a democracy, unlike a totalitarian state, is unafraid to conduct experiments in full view of all mankind. But the greatest lesson which we learned on this occasion was the unconquerable power of the human spirit. John Glenn taught us the value of raw courage, the importance of total commitment to a cause, and the significance of patriotism in a changing world. And he also taught us that the most compelling principle in life is not where a man is or where he came from, but what he is and where he is going.

Your curriculum expanded as you entered the Eleventh Grade. Now you could enroll in such classes as American history, speech, journalism, chemistry, and sociology as well as continue in English and Modern Languages. And you could make plans to serve as host in the Junior-Senior Prom. On the surface this appeared to be a quiet, uneventful year. No single dramatic incident could be highlighted as a particular moment to remember. Yet in subsequent years the great social movement which developed in the winter, spring, and summer of 1963 may have a far greater effect upon your lives than the election of President Kennedy or the flight of Colonel Glenn. Historians have already designated this period as the beginning of the great Negro Revolution.

On the centennial anniversary of the Emancipation Proclamation, the American Negro grew weary as he gazed at the world from his slums. One hundred years after he supposedly had received his freedom, he still did not have equal rights in education, housing, work opportunities, voting privileges, and entertainment facilities. As he brooded over his status he could see on his television screen leaders from the newly emerging countries in Africa take their place in the United Nations; he could see them voting on crucial world issues. Now he had become aware that twenty-three African nations had declared their independence since 1960. In doing so, they were, as one scholar recently observed, "leapfrogging from the 14th century to the 20th century, from the bullock-drawn cart directly to the jet plane." Such progress, though often accompanied with instability, impressed the American Negro and made him restless. Against this background of discontent and turmoil, the Negro was aroused and all America felt the reverberations. Thus in the second half of your junior year, a thousand cities trembled as the Negroes marched in the streets, sat on the sidewalks and in the cafés. Mass demonstrations had become their new weapon of power, and the jail their badge of courage. Not since the French Revolution of 1789, observed Martin Luther King, had so many people used the streets as a battleground. I saw them on August 28,

1963 as they came to the nation's capital, 200,000 strong. I stood on the street corner as they passed by on Constitution Avenue waving their banners in the warm summer breeze. I can still hear them now as they chanted the word "freedom" on the monument grounds, and then marched in unison toward the Lincoln Memorial. I could not help but feel as I witnessed this greatest single mass demonstration in America's history, that a revolution was underway. It was, in short, a revolution of nonviolent resistance which will perhaps continue for a generation to come.

We who are assembled here tonight cannot be untouched by the Negro's quest for freedom. We can, of course, condemn the crowds when they become overly militant and unruly. And we can indict the hatemongers who promote undue bitterness and hostility which all too often lead to extremism. But we must applaud the Negro's willingness to break the shackles of oppression and discrimination. Moreover, we must cheer his forceful effort to give new meaning to the maxim that "All men are created equal."

The Twelfth Grade serves as a bridge between high school and college, between classwork and employment opportunities. For many of you it represents the last year of formalized education before you enter society as a contributing citizen. To help prepare you for this challenge the school officials gave you an opportunity to study such subjects as government, physics, economics, typing, and stenography. In the third month of your senior year, while studying these new disciplines, you experienced your most dramatic moment to remember—a moment which gave you new insights in your required course of government. The date was November 22, 1963. President Kennedy, who was inaugurated while you were a freshman and who had not yet completed his third year in office, rode triumphantly down Main Street in Dallas on a good will tour. With his familiar bronzed look and ingratiating smile which exuded warmth and vigor, he waved to the jubilant crowds who had come to pay him tribute. As the motorcade approached the Texas Book Depository Building, the wife of Governor Connally turned to the President and said: "No one can say Dallas doesn't love and respect you." "You sure can't," he replied. These words, spoken at 12:30 P.M., were to be the last utterance of the man who today would have celebrated his forty-seventh birthday.

The details of his untimely assassination are too well known to recount here. A sorrowful and disbelieving nation bowed its head in penitence and asked the probing question "Why?" Why was a promising leader cut down in the flower of his youth? Why had a powerful democratic nation assassinated its fourth president in less than two hundred years? In search for an answer many, like Jack Ruby, found it easy to point an accusing finger at the fevered mind which pulled the trigger—Lee Harvey Oswald. Beneath the surface, however, rests a more alarming fact. If a sick man had committed the deed, uncontrolled hatred and intolerance had spawned it. And herein lies a great lesson for all of us. At best, hatred warps the mind and kills the spirit. At worst, it leads to violence and destruction.

Happily not all that occurred on that bleak November day was bad. We learned anew that our democratic form of government could withstand a severe shock. Indeed, so smooth was the transition from one leader to another that the world at large admired our strength and stability. As Americans rallied behind President Johnson they were to say with Abraham Lincoln: "Let us strive on to finish the work we are in; to bind up the nation's wounds."

Members of the graduating class of 1964, the four years which you have spent together in this hall of learning can never be forgotten. Here you sat in your classrooms approximately four thousand hours analyzing twenty to twenty-five different subjects. To get ready for these lectures and dialogues you worked an additional one thousand hours in your home. Through it all, living history has been your companion, your inspiration, and your guide. Future scholars may remember this brief span in your lives as "The Age of Kennedy," "The Space Age," or "The Negro Revolution." It is all of these. But it is more. It is an era in which man set his goals higher than he ever placed them before. No longer was he content to stand idly by while religious and racial intolerance flourished. No longer was he satisfied to stay earthbound while a limitless sky remained unexplored. These were noble challenges which called for heroic men.

As we receive our diplomas this evening let us bury those rationalizations which we have so often called into play in order to comfort ourselves in the face of failure. When we are tempted to bemoan our fate because obstacles are in our path, let us remember John

Fitzgerald Kennedy who rarely knew a moment without pain. When we are prone to downgrade our small hometown because it lacks the advantages of a large urban area, let us remember John Glenn. When we are quick to complain because there are those who discriminate against us, let us remember Martin Luther King. Together these gallant men have taught us to seek a cause in life. They have further taught us that total commitment to that cause transcends fear. Out of such courage and devotion a better America will emerge.

✿✿✿✿✿✿ **INDEX**